Inventing the PC

The MCM/70
Story

Zbigniew Stachniak

"*Inventing the PC* is a story that deserves
to be told. Most in the computer industry
believe that the personal computer was
either invented with the Altair – the
machine that got Bill Gates and Microsoft
started – or with the Apple computer of
Steve Jobs. Very few know about the
plethora of machines that appeared and
died in the mid-1970s. As this story is
located far from the current center of the
industry in California, it is especially
interesting."

DAVID ALAN GRIER, The Elliott School of
International Affairs, The George
Washington University

Inventing the PC

Zbigniew Stachniak

INVENTING
THE PC

THE MCM/70 STORY

McGill-Queen's University Press
Montreal & Kingston | London | Ithaca

© McGill-Queen's University Press 2011
ISBN 978-0-7735-3852-8

Legal deposit second quarter 2011
Bibliothèque nationale du Québec

Printed in Canada on acid-free paper that is 100% ancient forest free
(100% post-consumer recycled), processed chlorine free

This book has been published with the help of a grant from the Canadian
Federation for the Humanities and Social Sciences, through the Aid
to Scholarly Publications Program, using funds provided by the Social
Sciences and Humanities Research Council of Canada.

McGill-Queen's University Press acknowledges the support of the Canada
Council for the Arts for our publishing program. We also acknowledge the
financial support of the Government of Canada through the Canada Book
Fund for our publishing activities.

LIBRARY AND ARCHIVES CANADA
CATALOGUING IN PUBLICATION

Stachniak, Zbigniew, 1953–
Inventing the PC : the MCM/70 story / Zbigniew Stachniak.

Includes bibliographical references and index.
ISBN 978-0-7735-3852-8

1. MCM/70 (Computer).   2. Microcomputers – Canada – Design and
construction – History.   3. Computer engineering – Canada – History.
I. Title.

QA76.8.M43S73 2011   004.165   C2011-900297-3

Set in 10/14 Sabon with OCR A
Book design & typesetting by Garet Markvoort, zijn digital

TO THE MAKERS OF THE MCM/70

CONTENTS

ACKNOWLEDGMENTS

I wish to express my gratitude to many people who over the years have contributed to my research on Micro Computer Machines and who, through their donations, helped to build the MCM collection at the York University Computer Museum. I am particularly indebted to Mers Kutt for making his personal MCM archive available to me, for granting hours of interviews, and for enduring detailed questioning. To the late Kenneth Iverson I owe special thanks for the gift of his time and his invaluable recollections of APL's development at IBM.

A great debt of gratitude is due to former MCM employees who have supported my work through interviews, discussions, and donations of MCM documents and technical literature. André Arpin, Cam Farnell, Don Genner, Lorne Gladstone, José Laraya, Gordon Ramer, Reg Rea, Barrie Robinson, Glen Seeds, Morgan Smyth, and John Woods have offered not only their help through meetings and interviews but also their sincere encouragement for my MCM project. I wish to acknowledge helpful comments received from other former MCM employees and users of MCM products. Particular thanks go to David Borrowman, Ned Chapin, Ted Edwards, Haron Ezer, Mike Jenkins, J. Maika, Daniel Pimienta, Glenn Schneider, and John Wallace. For their recollections of early microprocessor development activities at Intel I would like to thank Marcian E. Hoff, Jr, Stanley Mazor, and Hal Feeney. I offer my thanks to William Kindree for long discussions on the history of the APL programming language and early mainframe computer industry.

Through the courtesy of Randall Brooks, vice-president, collections and research division of the Canada Science and Technology Museum Corporation, I had access to the museum's computer collection and could photograph some of the hardware to illustrate the book's narrative. Joyce Weisbecker brought to my attention her father's, Joseph Weisbecker's, outstanding contributions to computing. I'm also grateful to Alexander B. Magoun, executive director of the David Sarnoff Library, who made the Joseph Weisbecker archive available to me.

I especially wish to thank Christine McClymont for her invaluable editorial help and Joan Harcourt of the McGill-Queen's University Press who has provided unfailing support, encouragement, and professional guidance through the process that made the publication of my book possible.

Inventing the PC

INTRODUCTION

This book attempts to tackle one of the most intriguing issues in the modern history of computing – the dawn of the personal computer – not by comprehensive analysis of technological context and sociocultural environment, as is customarily done in the history of computing narratives, but through the details of a case study of a little-known company by the name of Micro Computer Machines (or MCM). In May 1973, MCM, a Toronto-based electronics company, publicly demonstrated the MCM/70 portable computer. Powered by a microprocessor and operated using a sophisticated programming language called APL, the MCM/70 was positioned to be a small, practical, general purpose computer for individual use. The MCM computer was meant to be affordable and as easy to use as a hand-held calculator. Nothing like it had ever been built before. Two years later, when the ideas of affordable computing began to crystallize into the personal computing paradigm, the MCM/70 computers were already espoused by Chevron Oil Research Company, Firestone, Toronto Hospital for Sick Children, Mutual Life Insurance Company of New York, Ontario Hydro-Electric Power Commission, NASA Goddard Space Flight Center, and the United States Army, to name just a few of the installations in North America.

The MCM/70 is possibly the earliest example of a microprocessor-powered computer (or microcomputer) designed and manufactured specifically for personal use. But despite being the forerunner of the personal computer of today, despite favourable reactions to its introduction from technology observers in Europe and North America, and regardless of its numerous installations (including many MCM/70s operated by the Computer Centre of the Soviet Academy of Sciences), the MCM computer's development has not, until recently, registered in the history of personal computing. Instead, the popular view has been that personal computing originated with the rise of the North American computer hobbyists' movement in the mid-1970s. According to this viewpoint, electronics enthusiasts, flocking around popular electronics magazines and, later, organized into computer clubs, were the ones who, in historian Paul Ceruzzi's words, "were willing to do the work needed to make microprocessor-based systems practical."[1]

If one accepts that only computer hobbyists were willing to work to make early microcomputers practical, then the history of personal computing could indeed be told without ever mentioning any of the microcomputer design activities that took place between the introduction of the world's first commercial microprocessor by Intel in the fall of 1971 and the advent of the microcomputer hobby movement in late 1974. However, that would eclipse not only the MCM/70 but also other practical early microcomputers such as the general purpose Micrals manufactured by the French company Réalisations et Études Électroniques (R2E) or Intel's microprocessor development systems.

To fend off the inevitable critics, I must stress that some computer historians have acknowledged at least the existence of mass-manufactured microcomputers, such as the R2E Micrals or Intel Intellecs, before 1975. However, they seem to have missed the significance of the early commercial microcomputer endeavours that took place almost concurrently in many parts of the world and almost as soon as news of the microprocessor burst from Intel. They seem to have overlooked the impact of the early systems activities at Intel and other semiconductor manufacturers on the rise of both the commercial and the hobby microcomputer industries.[2] Certainly, historical interpretations of many computing events will keep changing as time goes on and new information becomes available, and when the foundations on which some important historical conclusions are based undergo re-examination.

Mers Kutt, the inventor of the MCM/70 microcomputer and the first president of MCM, was never a part of the hobbyists' movement. Nor was he an idealistic hacker wrestling with the practicality of microcomputing problems. He was an inventor and an entrepreneur who embarked on the MCM/70 project in response to the problem of providing individuals with access to affordable computing on demand in areas such as business, research, and education. The MCM/70 was to fulfil the promise of the *personal computer* – the promise to extend and enrich one's intellectual and social abilities by means of an affordable, general-purpose computer for personal use. To that end, the computer was to be supported by a wide range of software – from the built-in high-level programming language and dedicated program libraries, to a text editor and, of course, computer games. It was to be a cost-effective and low-maintenance alternative to the high-performance minicomputers and time-sharing computer services that dominated the computer scene of the 1970s. Already in 1973, Kutt insisted that a dramatic shift in computer use from large mainframe computers to small microprocessor-based systems was inevitable.

The design of the MCM/70 began in early 1972, even before the first 8-bit microprocessor from Intel – the 8008, which was to be employed in Kutt's computer – was made available on the market. The first MCM/70 prototype was up and running a few months later and by mid-1973 the computer had been sent on its successful European tour to announce a new era of practical microprocessor-powered computers. It is evident that even before the microcomputer hobby movement began to form, MCM and other electronics companies, such as the French R2E, were actively pursuing the use of microprocessors in the design of low-cost, versatile, and practical computers. Therefore, to tell the story of the personal computer's creation and social acceptance accurately, it is essential to unlock the corporate histories of these early microcomputer companies.

This book is based in large part on the personal archive that Kutt assembled during his tenure at MCM. This collection consists of corporate documents, promotional materials, minutes of meetings, and letters and memos to and from the company's management, board of directors, employees, shareholders, clients, and suppliers. The most significant documents in the archive are the handwritten notes, a kind of personal corporate diary that Kutt kept from almost the first day of the MCM/70's development to the last day of his association with the company. The notes chronicle the development of the MCM/70 and detail both tasks accomplished and those still to be taken care of. They contain brief reports from various meetings and plans for upcoming events. Kutt made notes on technical novelties of the early 1970s and recorded the ever-changing financial situation of MCM and the marketing prospects for the MCM/70 computer. Finally, his notes constitute a log of the devastating power struggle between him and some of MCM's investors. In an interview for this book, Kutt described his note-taking habit as an entrepreneurial necessity. He explained that perhaps there were some successful entrepreneurs who could do their homework and still "have their offices looking pristine. I couldn't do that," concluded Kutt, "without my desk and office being paper all over."

Kutt's notes were a private matter, never intended for general distribution. One may therefore confidently conclude that they provide an untainted personal record of the birth of the personal computer concept at that critical point in the history of the semiconductor industry which is marked by the introduction of the microprocessor. Together with other documents in the archive, the notes offer a unique, insider's view of events that took place on the front line of pioneering work on microprocessor-based hardware. The documents chronicle the invention process and reveal people's thoughts, strategies, and plans. They show what information and options were available to MCM's engineering team: what they knew and didn't know, how well they understood what they were doing, and how that understanding shaped their decisions. Kutt's archive also captures the human dimension of an invention: entrepreneurial excitement, engineering ingenuity, and managerial commitment as well as the indecisiveness, carelessness, misjudgement, and over-reaching ambition that can so easily turn even the most promising venture into a missed opportunity.

But this book's narrative reflects more than just the single voice resounding through the pages of Kutt's notes. It also tries to build on the opinions and recollections of events as expressed by former MCM employees who directly participated in the design of the MCM/70 and its introduction into the market. These recollections and assessments of the events that took place at MCM in the early 1970s have helped me to piece together the complex, multi-dimensional structure of the MCM story. The interviews unearthed behind-the-scenes episodes of MCM's corporate life that were inaccessible to Kutt and therefore could not find their way into his notes. These same interviews, however, also revealed inevitable lapses in the way people report past events: the incompleteness and local inconsistencies, and the emotional filters applied to the selection and assessment of the episodes that mattered. But such is the nature of human memory: it annotates events with personal emotions, preferences, and attitudes. With the passing of time, the details of episodes may fade from memory and these psychological trappings become the only things that remain. The story of the making of the MCM/70 as chronicled in the pages of this book does not strip away human emotions from the events. However, it does clearly demarcate the emotional and factual boundaries of MCM's corporate history.

And now we are ready to begin. The year is 1971, the place, Toronto, Canada. There are no personal computers on the consumer market yet – but one will soon be in the making.

1

At the Beginning, There Were Two

In the fall of 1971 in Toronto, Merslau (Mers) Kutt, a well-known Canadian entrepreneur, met Gordon Ramer, a software engineer and the assistant director of the York University Computer Centre, to chat about computer technology.

The two had briefly met three years earlier, at Queen's University in Kingston, Ontario, where Kutt was the director of the university's computer centre. It was a brief and apparently inconsequential meeting following a lecture, organized by Queen's, that had attracted Ramer strongly enough to make the 260-kilometre trip from York University, on the outskirts of Toronto. By the fall of 1971, things were entirely different. A project that Ramer had completed recently at York was of great interest to Kutt. For some time, Kutt had been nursing an invention in his mind that, when developed and properly marketed, might have a profound effect on the computer industry and the social status of computing. But Kutt didn't have all the essential aspects of his invention solved. He thought Ramer's expertise could be just what he needed.

In the early 1970s, the consumer electronics market was going through one of the hottest periods in its history. Advancements in microelectronics, especially in integrated circuit technologies, had made it possible to offer inexpensive desktop and, soon after, hand-held and pocket-sized digital electronic calculators. It wasn't so much the "cigarette pack" size or the aesthetically pleasing plastic cases that attracted people to these new gadgets. It was the idea of a personal calculator, of a powerful, inexpensive calculating device for your own unrestricted use, always in your pocket, in your briefcase, or on your desk. In 1971, the promise of calculator power at your fingertips (pledged by Bowmar Instrument Corporation, Canon, Commodore Business Machines, and, soon after, by scores of other calculator manufacturers) was rapidly gaining social acceptance.

What Kutt had in mind, however, was even bigger than the pocket calculator. The effect of his invention on society was to be even more profound than the replacement of slide rules and electro-mechanical calculating devices with tiny battery-powered calculators whose dimensions were constrained only by the size of the keypad and the display. What Kutt wanted to build was a "personal computer" – an inexpensive, small, digital, general-purpose computer owned and operated by an individual. These personal computers would make the individual an even freer person, with computing – not merely calculating – power at his or her disposal, whether in an office, a research lab, or a classroom.

At the time of Kutt's meeting with Ramer in Toronto, the world of computing consisted exclusively of large and expensive mainframe computers and smaller, but also expensive, minicomputers. In 1971, there were 3,548 computers of all types in Canada: 1,814 in the province of Ontario, 764 in Quebec, and only four in tiny Prince Edward Island.[1] The mainframes and "minis" of the early 1970s were never intended to function as personal computers – in fact, in those days, the expression "personal computer" wasn't even an academic term. Computer services were intended to support not individual use but the computational needs of governmental agencies, corporations, and research and academic institutes. The high cost of computer rentals, maintenance, and operation was passed on to customers and that significantly limited the use of computers by small and medium-sized companies.

Kutt foresaw a very different future for computing than did the major computer manufacturers. A practical, inexpensive, and easy-to-operate personal computer, in his view, would make computing on demand the bread and butter of many human activities in areas such as business, finance, and education as well as research, engineering, data entry, and processing. In the not so distant future, he speculated, there would be only a limited number of large computers in use but millions of small PCs in the hands of individuals, much like glorified pocket calculators.

Kutt was convinced that this dramatic reshaping of the computer scene would be brought about by the microprocessor, a revolutionary new device that Intel Corporation of Santa Clara, California, was about to introduce into the market. In November 1970, Kutt met Robert Noyce – co-founder and first CEO of Intel – during the Fall Joint Computer Conference in Houston, Texas. Both Intel and Consolidated Computer Incorporated (CCI), which Kutt had incorporated in 1969, were just two young start-up companies, blazing trails in the computer and semiconductor markets. In the clichéd scene of a conference recess in a cocktail bar, Noyce and Kutt were passionately sharing ideas, using napkins to draw specifications of a new gadget – an 8-bit microprocessor – that Intel was developing for Computer Terminal Corporation and that Kutt wanted for novel data entry products developed by CCI. But even though CCI was rapidly gaining an international reputation, Kutt never saw the introduction of microprocessor technology into CCI products. A few months after his meeting with Noyce, he was forced out of CCI in rather murky circumstances.

It was through the application of microprocessor technology that Kutt hoped to achieve the hardware objectives of his new,

Mers Kutt (left) and Gordon Ramer (right) in 1973. (Source: York University Computer Museum, photographer unknown.)

post-CCI, venture into low-cost computer systems. Reassured by Noyce that Intel's first 8-bit microprocessor – the 8008 – would soon see the light, Kutt was left with only one unresolved problem – software. Not just any software, but a suite of computer programs that would make his PC as easy to use as a desktop calculator. And that is why he needed Ramer and his intimate knowledge of the programming language called APL.

Ramer's long-lasting affection for the APL language had begun with his 1968 trip to Queen's University to attend a lecture given by APL's inventor, Kenneth Iverson. Since joining IBM's Research Division in Yorktown Heights, New York, Iverson had acquired a unique status among the software engineering crowd at IBM, as well as outside the company, for his novel views on formal languages in relation to computing. But it was not until 1968 that IBM made the APL software (in the form of the APL\360 interpreter of Iverson's APL language) publicly available, cost-free but without any formal support. The APL lecture at Queen's was therefore a unique opportunity to learn about the language from the inventor himself.

Ramer returned to York University enchanted: "I guess that was just something that really tickled my fancy and I fell in love with the language."[2] He was not the first or the last software engineer to feel so strongly about the APL language. For him and many others, the fascination of APL was not only its syntactic simplicity, conciseness, and expressivity, but also Iverson himself and his programming language philosophy. "I can remember being absolutely blown away," continued Ramer. "Coming from a mathematical and computer (Fortran/Cobol/360 Assembler) background, I found APL elegant and logical. Finally, you could make the computer do the things you wanted without having to jump through hoops to talk the computer's language."

Ramer's interest in computers had started in the early 1960s when he entered the Applied Science in Electrical Engineering program at the University of Waterloo in Waterloo, Ontario. At that time the only computer on campus was an IBM 610.

> This [computer] looked like a desk with an attached typewriter – a one-user-at-a-time system. I soon switched my hours in the computer lab to midnight, to 2 or 3 A.M., so I wouldn't have to line up. I remember the instructor for the course, Wes Graham, saying to me near the end of the term that I must not have much interest in this area because he never saw me in the computer lab. My response was to ask him to drop in at midnight, but he never showed up at that time, nor did he again question my commitment.

Ramer graduated from Waterloo in 1964. Four years later, he was attending Iverson's talk at Queen's – one of the most influential lectures in his professional career.

To explain the impact of APL on Ramer, it is necessary to switch the narrative focus temporarily onto Kenneth E. Iverson himself. He was born in 1920 and grew up on a small farm in Camrose, Alberta. From childhood on, he expressed an interest in and demonstrated a talent for mathematics. However, at age thirteen, he came to the conclusion that high school was useful only for would-be teachers, and he certainly didn't find teaching appealing. Consequently, having little educational guidance at home, he quit school and went to work on a farm.

In 1946, Iverson was a twenty-six-year-old veteran of the Second World War entering university in search of a new life. Within a few years, he received his Bachelor of Arts degree in Mathematics and Physics from Queen's University and, soon after, was awarded a scholarship to do graduate work at Harvard University. One of the first courses that Iverson took at Harvard was taught by Howard Hathaway Aiken. "To me, it [Aiken's course] was a revelation," said Iverson. "It was the first time when I encountered a course or a professor who suggested that there were still useful things that can be done."

Aiken's classes were packed. He was not only a first-rate scholar and the director of Harvard's Computation Laboratory, but also a renowned designer and builder of digital "electronic brains." When Iverson first stepped onto Harvard's campus, Aiken had four powerful calculating machines to his credit – named Mark I, II, III, and IV and conceived between 1937 and 1950. Under Aiken, and using Aiken's Mark IV computer, Iverson completed his doctoral work in 1954. Soon after, he started his independent work on a symbolic language to be known as "Iverson notation."

The origin of Iverson's notation was the Automated Data Processing program that Aiken instituted at Harvard and that Iverson was a part of, which focused on the applied side of computing and on computer education. While teaching and writing a book on automated data processing, Iverson realized that to explain concepts such as sorting algorithms concisely, he needed an expanded system of notation – a system both simpler and

Kenneth Iverson deliver-
ing his lecture "Teaching
APL" during the 1980 APL
Users' Meeting in Toronto.
(Source: York University
Computer Museum,
photographer unknown.)

more general than conventional mathematical notation could
provide. "The mathematical notation that I had been raised
on just wasn't adequate," explained Iverson. "So I turned my
attention to notation. And having had in my [doctoral] thesis
work experience in implementing things on a computer, I always thought, as I developed notation, I always had in mind
that this is something that should be actually implemented. So
that's what started me on what became APL."

Iverson notation had its roots in conventional mathematical
practice. "I used accepted mathematical notations unchanged,"
Iverson remarked in a July 1977 interview for *Electronic Design*.
"I was perfectly happy with the conventional +, -, ×, and \ used
in grade school and up."[3] But as he went from one application
to another, he found needs and reasons to expand the conventional notation by introducing new symbols.

For Iverson, a notation system was an essential tool of thought,
a systematic and unambiguous foundation for precise and efficient reasoning. Essentially, Iverson notation was a mathemat-

ical notation that permitted the expression of concepts and methods in a very compact and unambiguous way. Of course, he was aware that similar ideas, such as those at the foundation of symbolic logic, had been powering modern mathematics and physics for quite some time. The novelty of Iverson's approach was to view notation not only as a formal language for doing applied mathematics – that is, for defining and proving properties of mathematical procedures of interest to a scientist – but also as a programming language whose sentences could be used to implement these procedures and to execute them on a computer. In short, what Iverson was searching for was a notation system in which the descriptive and analytical power of a mathematical language could naturally coexist with the executability and universality of a programming language. In his 1979 ACM Turing Award lecture, Iverson summarized this in the following way: "The advantages of executability and universality found in programming languages can be effectively combined, in a single coherent language, with the advantages offered by mathematical notation."[4]

Unable to convert his teaching position at Harvard into a tenured appointment, Iverson moved to IBM in 1960, where he continued to work on his notation system with a group of people that included Philip Abrams, Lawrence Breed, and Adin Falkoff. In 1965, their work resulted in the first complete implementation of Iverson's notation as a programming language done by Abrams and Breed. The language itself was baptized "APL" by Falkoff, who derived the name from the title of Iverson's book *A Programming Language*, published in 1962. In this book, Iverson described the principles and applications of his notation system.

After some dispute with IBM's Applied Physics Lab, which objected to the acronym, the name "APL" was cleared by IBM and would soon mesmerize a large number of computer pro-

From left to right: Dick Lathwell, Kenneth Iverson, Roger Moore, Adin Falkoff, Philip Abrams, and Lawrence Breed during the 1978 APL Users' Meeting. This photograph appeared in *I.P. Sharp Newsletter* 6, no. 6 (1978) with the caption "it is believed to be the first time that all six 'originators of APL' have been in the same place at the same time, it is probably the first time that all six have worn jackets and ties simultaneously and the first time that Ken and Adin have been observed to smile simultaneously." (Source: York University Computer Museum, photographer unknown.)

grammers across North America and beyond. In the 1970s, APL conferences and meetings, publications and interest groups, as well as "I Love APL" stickers and buttons, T-shirts and songs, transformed the initial curiosity about the principles of APL programming developed at IBM into an unprecedented cultural phenomenon, rivaled only by the strength, creativity, and enthusiasm of the North American computer hobbyists' movement of the time.

Mers Kutt and Gordon Ramer were devoted converts to APL. It was Kutt who, in his capacity as the director of the Queen's Computing Centre, invited Iverson to deliver his 1968 lecture. Both Kutt and Ramer appreciated the language's strengths: its expressive power and the compactness and simplicity of its syntax. What wasn't clear to Ramer – yet! – was by what magic of hardware engineering a small and inexpensive computer, such as the one envisioned by Kutt, could function with sufficient power and memory to execute APL programs. In 1971, APL was commercially available only on mainframe computers, and for good reason: these machines were fast and could be equipped with enough memory to support multiple APL users. Of course, mainframes were also very big and very expensive. And now Kutt wanted his computer to be not only tiny and cheap but also APL programmable!

While chatting with Kutt about the technical specifications of Intel's 8008 microprocessor, Ramer was deeply skeptical, at first, about building an APL computer around the 8008 chip. "First time we met," recollected Kutt, "he [Ramer] thought that I was from another world ... putting APL into that? No way!" What was worse, Kutt could not even present a sample of the 8008 chip to Ramer. At the time of their meeting in fall 1971, the processor was still in development and wouldn't be available on the market until April of the following year. Kutt could, however, disclose the device's specifications: its processing speed and the amount of memory with which the processor could directly operate. "Mers had a vision of APL running on this Intel 8008 chip," recalled Ramer, "and that took a very big leap of faith in those days, because this was an eight-bit machine which chugged away at some incredibly slow speed."

Looking at the Intel 8008's specifications, Ramer's main concern, apart from the low processing speed of the chip, was the insufficient amount of memory the processor could operate with directly – just 16K (kilobytes). The popular APL\360 language required 32K just to provide a user with a space to write and execute programs, not to mention the memory required to store the APL\360 interpreter itself or for the host computer to perform other computational tasks. The 32K of memory were twice as much as the Intel 8008 could directly support, and much more than a typical mini of the 1960s was equipped with (the immensely popular PDP-8 minicomputer manufactured by Digital Equipment Corporation was shipped with just 4,096 twelve-bit words of memory in its basic configuration).

Kutt, of course, was aware of the insufficient memory problem. A simple calculation left no doubt that, without creative hardware and software solutions, the task of creating an APL computer to run on the Intel 8008 chip was simply impossible. For a start, an APL computer would require approximately 16K of memory to store APL. An additional 20K were required to provide the user with a workspace – a section of computer memory where all the user's APL work would be done. And, finally, another 8K or so were needed so the computer's operating system could take care of display, external storage of data and programs, and other functions. The total of 44K was almost three times what the 8008 processor could support directly. This is why Kutt wanted to meet Ramer. Ramer was not only one of the first software engineers in Canada to successfully develop and implement a dialect of APL, but his version of the language, named York APL, was memory efficient and sported a number of unique features.

In 1968, the York University Computer Centre, where Ramer was employed as assistant director, operated an IBM System 360 model 40 mainframe computer. The only APL software that could be installed on it was the APL\360 interpreter just made publicly available by IBM. In spite of a growing enthusiasm for APL in its computer centre, York University could not afford to install APL\360. The software would consume all the computational resources that their model of the 360 mainframe

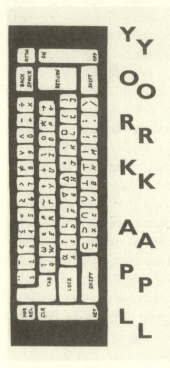

York APL reference card, 1972. (Source: York University Special Collections.)

could provide. In short, under APL\360, York's computer would become a dedicated APL machine unable to support any non-APL users. "There was no way that York could afford anything like that," said Ramer. "So I started out in my spare time to write an [APL] interpreter and I actually got the thing running within a year. And it was running well enough that we could supply APL to a few people [simultaneously], so it became fairly useful."

York APL was a clever reworking of APL\360. Due to its low memory requirements, it could coexist with other software installed on a modest mainframe computer. This, and other unique features not offered by APL\360, such as file manipulation functions and the ability to communicate with the operating system, attracted a number of universities and research institutions that operated mainframe computers of a similar configuration to that installed at York.[5] What Kutt wanted from Ramer was not only a new, highly memory-efficient APL language but also a memory management system that could overcome the twenty-eight-kilobyte memory deficit.

Ramer recognized that almost everything in Kutt's proposal was uncharted territory, from defining and building to actually marketing the personal computer of the future. In Ramer's own field of expertise, no one had ever developed and implemented a high-level programming language, such as APL, to run on a microprocessor. He had to admit, however, that Kutt's ideas, if successfully realized, could open up a new and potentially vast market of small personal computers. And, of course, they could both become very rich, very fast. This was probably why Ramer agreed to team up with Kutt.

On 28 December 1971 Mers Kutt incorporated Kutt Systems Incorporated (KSI) in Toronto, with the purpose of designing, building, and marketing a small APL computer. Kutt became the president of KSI, and Ramer, who offered the rights to York APL in exchange for 30,000 common shares of KSI, assumed the sole responsibility for equipping the computer with APL software. Their computer would be known as the MCM/70. It was unveiled in 1973 to thunderous applause from the technical and popular press in North America and Europe. The era of personal computing was about to begin.

   But before any of the MCM/70s would be shipped out to its users, KSI (renamed as Micro Computer Machines) would have to weather prolonged corporate turmoil – from a devastating power struggle and employee revolt to personal resignations and financial collapse.

2

Inventing the PC

The idea of creating a small desktop computer for personal use did not occur to Kutt suddenly. It was, rather, an evolutionary process powered by his expert knowledge of the computer field, his innate technical curiosity, and, most of all, by his cease-less search for new ways of making people's interaction with computers more user-friendly in large organizations such as universities.

Kutt knew and understood academia as well as he did the computer business. He had earned his Bachelor of Arts degree in Mathematics and Physics from the University of Toronto in 1956. After graduation, he did some electronic circuit design and analysis work at the Advanced Development Laboratory of Philips Electronics Industries Ltd, but soon moved to IBM Canada as an applied science representative. It was not only IBM's computer technology that mesmerized him. "In about the second week up there [at IBM]," recalled Kutt, "I'm having lunch with a branch manager and a bunch of customer people, getting a shrimp cocktail, which I don't think I'd ever had in my life, roast beef, prime rib, I'm into a new world!" It was a new world indeed for twenty-four-year-old Kutt – a sharp contrast with the not-so-distant past when, at age eight, "he was selling newspapers at three cents apiece at the corner of Dundas and Spadina."[1]

Kutt's career took off when he joined Honeywell Controls Ltd in 1959. His natural talent for salesmanship and his enthusiasm for technological advancement, coupled with his understanding of market needs, shortly made him the company's top salesman in western Canada. That success later put him in charge of all Honeywell's computer activities in eastern Canada. The Honeywell experience would prove invaluable in future ventures which required attracting talented personnel, obtaining development capital, and securing crucial sales contracts.

But at thirty-two, after six years at Honeywell, he realized that he would never be able to satisfy his research and development ambitions if he stayed with the company. In 1965, in a rather sudden move, he gave up his lucrative position at Honeywell, and joined Queen's University as a professor of mathematics. Queen's – one of Canada's oldest and best-known universities – was far behind other Canadian universities in the area of academic computing. Kutt was hired to change that. "I had carte blanche to just get things going, the least of which was to get the professors to use the [university's] computer and not be afraid."

When Kutt arrived at Queen's, the university's computer resources comprised an IBM 1620 Data Processing System interfaced with a printer and a punch card input/output device, most likely an IBM 1622 Card Read Punch. The 1620 was IBM's popular early computer for small businesses, academic research, and engineering applications. The computer itself wasn't particularly slow. On the other hand, the process of data and program entry into the computer certainly was. Kutt recalls students and faculty lining up in the university's computer center to have their computer programs executed.

But executing a program on the 1620 computer wasn't a simple matter. First, a user's program and data had to be converted into a deck of paper cards – punch cards – using the IBM 1622 Card Read Punch. The computer console's typewriter was used to type data or program lines, with each key-press resulting

The IBM 1620 Data Processing System was a popular early computer for small businesses, academic research, and engineering applications. (Courtesy of the Canada Science and Technology Museum, photograph by Z. Stachniak.)

in a mechanically punched hole in a specific place on a card. Different patterns of holes on each card represented different pieces of data or sections of the program. Therefore the order of cards in the resulting deck was as important as the information punched into them. Finally, the deck of cards was fed to the computer for execution. When there were multiple users waiting for access to the computer, their jobs, already residing on punch cards, would not be executed on a first-come-first-served basis, but batched together by an operator. Only when there were enough jobs in a batch were they submitted for processing.

If a submitted program contained errors, the owner was informed about them only after the batch containing the erroneous program had been processed. To correct the errors, the owner had to punch a new deck of cards and, again, hand it over to an operator to be batched with scores of other jobs. The

IBM punch card. (Source: York University Computer Museum.)

process continued until such time as the owner was happy with the program and the results of its execution.

The batch-processing of computer jobs was especially popular on large mainframe computers such as the IBM\360. Computer time was expensive, and the batch mode utilization of mainframes was a widely used way of reducing costs.

Shortly after Kutt's arrival at Queen's, the university replaced its aging 1620 computer with a modern IBM\360 model 40 and, later, upgraded it to a model 50. Kutt also introduced Queen's to the APL language. Students and faculty interested in APL had access to several dedicated APL terminals that they could use to connect to the university's computer for their computational needs. For non-APL users, punch cards and the batching of computer jobs continued.

Historically, punch cards were among the oldest and most prevalent computer input media. Supplying an extended line of hardware to punch, read, and process cards was also a lucrative business for companies such as IBM. However, already, at Honeywell, Kutt had gained a clear idea of how to make computer data entry easier without the need of punch cards. One could simply provide programmers or data entry personnel with a computer terminal consisting primarily of a keyboard and a display. The keyed information could be stored on an external memory medium such as a magnetic drum or magnetic tape. The host computer would then pick up the stored information directly from that external memory, rather than wait for the deck of sorted cards to be punched and fed into it.

There were significant advantages to such an arrangement. Before processing, the data keyed in by an operator could be verified, updated, deleted, or even sorted and combined with other data already saved in the system's memory. There would be no need for expensive punch card equipment such as card readers, punchers, or sorters. In addition, multiple terminals could be connected to a single host computer. But, as Kutt used to say, "You have to look at the practical side of the development. You cannot build something just because it is neat." He had to wait until the mid-1960s for the Key-Edit system, as he called his first invention, to become an economically sound concept. Then magnetic drums and tapes came down in cost, and Digital Equipment Corporation introduced the PDP-8 minicomputer – a small computer that Kutt needed to control all the operations of the terminals of his data entry system.

"My arrangement [with Queen's] was that I'd be able to set up my own company in parallel," said Kutt, "without jeopardizing my own position in the department. I had already developed the idea of a key-to-drum product and wanted to bring such a product to the marketplace."[2]

While at Queen's, Kutt teamed up with Donald Pamenter to form his first Company, Consolidated Computer Services Ltd (incorporated in 1969 under the name of Consolidated Computer Inc.), to develop and manufacture a novel, fully computerized data entry system named the Key-Edit 100. Multiple data entry terminals of the Key-Edit (called key-stations) were connected to a shared PDP-8 minicomputer which controlled all the data entry and editing functions of the Key-Edit. Almost

Consolidated Computer Falcon Key-Edit Business Information System. (Source: Consolidated Computer Inc. promotional brochure, York University Computer Museum.)

overnight, CCI became one of the most innovative and internationally recognized Canadian high tech companies of that period. "The biggest thing was to get a big sale," recollected Kutt, "and I used to camp out down at General Motors in Detroit and worked at getting them. We got them and ... from there, the Key-Edit really took off and people knew it around the world."

By the end of the 1970s, CCI had installed over 30,000 keystations of its Key-Edit system in twenty-eight countries. Other companies that soon followed CCI with similar key-edit products sold or rented even more systems. The era of punch cards was over, just like that. The Canadian press called CCI Canada's Computer Company and the symbol of Canada's challenge for a share of the worldwide computer market.[3]

By June of 1969, Kutt was out of Queen's and devoting all his time to CCI. That year he was also elected president of the Canadian Information Processing Society. But the satisfaction of having a breakthrough product and getting a taste of managing a successful company did not last long. In the fall of 1971, he was squeezed out of CCI for reasons best explained in a separate publication. (One would have to deal with a vast range of issues, from raising and managing large capital to the incompetence of some top bureaucrats in the Canadian federal government, to name just two.) That year, he was also struck by personal tragedy. A few months before his departure from CCI, he lost his wife to cancer.

It was also in the fall of 1971 that Kutt started to focus all his technical and entrepreneurial expertise on a new invention – a desktop APL computer. Several factors shaped the new direction of his interest and the process of this computer's invention. Yes, Kutt had indeed created a better computing environment at Queen's University, but the APL terminals connected to the shared IBM\360 computer were still slow as they had to share the computer's resources. Things would be different entirely if they could be turned into stand-alone computers. Yes, his Key-Edit system did away entirely with punch cards, but it could be improved considerably if the key-stations became more independent, a bit like little computers themselves. And finally, there was the APL programming language and the microprocessor. For Kutt, there could be only one result of the integration of all these factors: a microprocessor-based desktop computer running APL. "I knew that this was going to be a computer of the future," explained Kutt, "and [with] one per person, no need to time share. And on the way there, APL – such a powerful language ... I saw what APL did to the university."

Since the incorporation of KSI, Kutt had been keeping detailed design notes documenting his microcomputer project. From these documents it is possible to reconstruct the main fea-

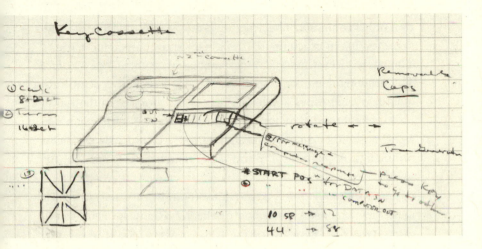

This drawing of the Key-Cassette is among the oldest preserved sketches of a microcomputer designed for the consumer market. (Source: M. Kutt's archive.)

tures of his "computer of the future." The notes leave no doubt that the new semiconductor products from Intel and the success of pocket and desktop electronic calculators on the consumer market had a major impact on Kutt. "The world was full of calculators," recollected Kutt. "They made a real Big Bang." Initially, Kutt was of the opinion that a prototype, at least, of the APL computer could be made by KSI from off-the-shelf calculator components. In his notes, Kutt remarked: "Try and use existing calculator cover, display, modify power supply, and replace keyboard." Indeed, off-the-shelf calculator components would save his young company money. For example, a computer case matching the design elegance of a typical desktop calculator cover would have to be manufactured using injection molding. But that was an expensive process: a good quality mould with sharp corners would cost around $25,000.

Kutt's notes also contain an unusual drawing in which he depicted the "Key-Cassette" device, undoubtedly the first incarnation of his computer. The drawing is among the oldest preserved sketches of a microcomputer designed for the consumer market. The name "Key-Cassette" most likely derives from "Key-Edit." The drawing depicts a case in the style of a typical desktop calculator of that time. The lower part of the front panel houses a built-in keyboard. The top part contains a cassette drive on the right, and either an acoustic coupler or a second cassette drive on the left. A small display and some switches are placed in the middle of the panel.

The annotated drawing provides enough information to let us grasp the basic operations of the Key-Cassette. The small thirty-two-key keyboard of the Key-Cassette would allow the user to enter all the alphanumeric and numeric characters as well as the APL and special function symbols. To achieve such compactness, each key was designed to enter up to five symbols (using a combination of keystrokes). The symbols on the keys would be colour-coded to distinguish between symbols that could be entered directly (red marks in the center of the keys) and those that could be entered via a combination of keystrokes (black marks placed in the corners of the keys).

The one-line display of the Key-Cassette would allow the user to view a single line of APL code, a computer output, or an error message. The rotate keys "←" and "→" would allow moving the displayed information left and right to reveal it fully, and the roll keys "↓" and "↑" would allow scrolling through the lines of APL code. The sketch of the Key-Cassette is augmented with two drawings of possible segmented display elements, one comprised of thirteen display segments and the other of fifteen segments. Finally, the tape cassette drives were to provide external storage.

But that was early in 1972. The production model of the MCM/70 developed two years later shared a number of features with the Key-Cassette concept: the one-line display, the built-in

Berkeley Associates
Simon computer
on the front page
of the October
1950 issue of
Radio-Electronics.

keyboard, and the cassette drive. It was, however, a different product entirely.

In 1971, the idea of a computer dedicated to personal use wasn't new. There were other inventors who had designed their computing devices for personal or educational use long before Kutt started to work on his PC. In the late 1940s, Edmund Berkeley, a great enthusiast of computing and computer education, conceived his first small relay-based computing device and named it Simon. Berkeley published its design between 1950 and 1951 in a series of articles in *Radio-Electronics* magazine. The "World's Smallest Electric Brain" was a digital but, at the same time, very primitive computer operating with only four numbers: 0, 1, 2, and 3. But Berkeley designed his "little idiot," as he referred to Simon, not as a scientific tool but as an educational aid "to exhibit in simple understandable form the essential principle of any artificial brain."[4]

Berkeley's ideas inspired others to explore ways of bringing knowledge of computers and their role in modern society to the attention of educators, electronics hobbyists, and even children.

One such person was Joseph Weisbecker, an RCA computer development engineer. His computer career spanned many areas, from the design of mainframe computer hardware to microprocessor and microcomputer architectures. But demystifying the little-understood world of digital computing, and making computers part of everyday experience, was his true passion, an enthusiasm that he picked up from Berkeley. "When my father read Edmund Berkeley's book *Giant Brains*," explained Weisbecker's daughter Joyce,

he saw for the first time what an electronic computer could do, but, more importantly, *how* it worked. Binary logic, flip-flops, switching circuits – very simple elements combined in subtle, clever ways resulted in surprisingly sophisticated behavior from a machine. And, better than mechanical gears and levers, this machine could be made to completely change its behavior without rebuilding it. Now *this* was magic!

By the end of the 1960s, Weisbecker's interest in computer education and low-cost computing converged into a computer concept that he referred to as a Flexible Recreational and Educational Device, or FRED. Weisbecker envisioned FRED not as yet another computer toy, like the many he had designed in the past, but as a real, minimum-cost, general-purpose computer for home and school applications. "Everything that my father did with computers was an attempt to get as much of a FRED

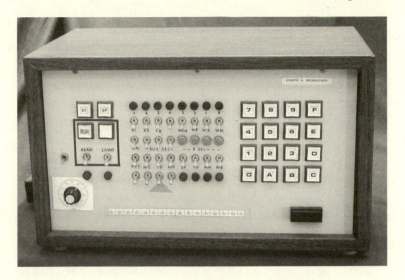

Weisbecker's System oo computer. (Courtesy of the David Sarnoff Library, photograph by Z. Stachniak.)

computer into hobbyists' and children's hands as possible," said Joyce Weisbecker. "In this sense, even his 'computer' books (the one that played Tic-Tac-Toe against you and the one that read your mind) were early versions of FRED, as were *Think-A-Dot* [computer toy] and the *Computer Coin Games* book."[5]

As a hardware concept, FRED went through a number of design phases due to the technological realities at RCA. Its first incarnation was the System oo built by Weisbecker in 1971 at RCA Labs in Princeton, NJ. Its design called for the FRED microprocessor, an 8-bit single-chip processor capable of directly accessing 64K of memory. Weisbecker designed the microprocessor in 1971 and originally presented its architecture in the RCA technical report *An Eight-Bit Micro-Processor*. The FRED microprocessor was more capable than any of the microprocessors being developed at Intel at that time. Unfortunately for Weisbecker, in 1971 RCA did not have the technology to make the FRED chip a reality. He would have to wait until 1974 for the two-chip realization of his processor, and until 1976 for its single-chip implementation. By then RCA wasn't calling it FRED, but the COSMAC microprocessor.

Although System 00 never went into production, Weisbecker continued his efforts to interest RCA in his FRED ideas. In one of his 1972 memos he writes: "FRED is an exciting new consumer product possibility. For the first time, a full power electronic computer could be available at the price of a hi-fi system or colour TV. Every home and classroom is a potential customer."[6] The low cost of FRED was to be achieved by designing its hardware around the single-chip FRED microprocessor, using an ordinary TV set as the display monitor and an audio cassette player to store and retrieve data and programs. But in the early 1970s, RCA was more interested in his microprocessor than in the new reincarnations of FRED that Weisbecker continued to design; FRED 1, FRED 1.5, and FRED 2 existed only as prototypes, and, outside of RCA, only Weisbecker's daughters had the opportunity to use some of them in their home.

Finally, in 1974, FRED found its way into the catalogues of RCA consumer Electronics products. First, it became the RCA MicroTutor – a little microcomputer used by RCA to showcase its COSMAC microprocessor architecture. Then, in 1977, it became the RCA COSMAC VIP single-board microcomputer and the Studio II programmable game console, one of the earliest of its type on the consumer market. In 1976, Weisbecker offered the smallest of the FREDs to the computer hobbyists. He named it ELF and published its design in a three-part article in *Popular Electronics*.[7]

The FRED microprocessor earned Weisbecker the prestigious RCA David Sarnoff Outstanding Achievement Award "for the design of a new computer architecture appropriate for mass production of microprocessors." Realized as the RCA CDP1802 COSMAC microprocessor, it paved RCA's way into the lucrative microprocessor-powered consumer electronics market, which would soon be full of FRED-like offerings. Since 1977, a fast-growing number of both well-established and new manufacturers of consumer electronics products had introduced scores of low-cost FRED-like microcomputers for home and educational applications. As predicted by Weisbecker, they were useful and very popular. As an example, the sales of the VIC-20, a low-cost computer introduced by Commodore in 1980, reached the one million mark in early 1983, when Commodore was shipping 100,000 units a month.

But more than a decade earlier, in 1971, Kutt embarked on his microcomputer project with a vision worlds apart from Weisbecker's FRED philosophy. Kutt didn't intend to develop yet another educational toy for demonstrating the principles of digital logic, or to manufacture a minimum-cost computer for a limited range of applications at home or classroom. He wasn't into hobby computing, either, despite the computer hobbyists' movement, which had been growing in strength since Stephen B. Gray founded the Amateur Computer Society (ACS) in 1966 and began publishing the ACS *Newsletter* for computer enthusiasts and experimenters.

Instead, Kutt wanted to build a practical, versatile, and inexpensive desktop computer to satisfy the computational needs of individuals in business, research, and education, at a fraction of the cost charged by typical time-sharing computer service companies. In his opinion, low-cost microcomputers, such as the one he intended to build, would allow the cost-effective use of computers in many new fields of application. And, finally, a user-friendly and easy-to-comprehend computer operating environment was as critical to his project as small size and battery operation was to the pocket calculator.

While Kutt's concept of an APL computer looked sound from a marketing point of view, turning it into an economically feasible product relied on a number of assumptions. One of them was that the rapid progress in semiconductor technologies would lead swiftly to inexpensive and high-capacity memory devices. The core memory routinely used in mainframes and mini-computers was large and inappropriate for Kutt's computer. The first semiconductor memory chips were small but, unfortunately, they were also expensive and of low capacity. For instance, the Intel 1101 random access memory (RAM) chip was a tiny device (less than a centimetre in length and less than half a centimetre wide) but it could hold only 256 bits of information. If a computer's RAM capacity were to be, say, 64,000 bits (i.e., eight thousand 8-bit words or 8K), then its RAM board would have to contain two hundred and fifty 1101 chips. In 1971, at a cost of, say, $12 a chip, that would add up to $3,000 – or the equivalent of a new Ford Grande Mustang with a vinyl top and a Grande logo beside the rear window! One of the early Intel bestsellers – the 2102 RAM chip, which would be eventually employed in the MCM/70 – had a memory capacity of four 1101 chips. But in 1973, one had to pay $20 per chip, or $1,280 to populate the same 8K RAM board.[8] There were other problems: external storage, display, and APL software.

Of course, the biggest gamble of the enterprise was the assumption that the 8008 microprocessor, or one of its successors, if ever developed, would be able to reliably support all the functions of Kutt's computer. The first commercially available microprocessor, the Intel 4004, was introduced in November of 1971. The processor, together with three supporting chips, was designed by Intel for a Japanese client and was meant to be used in a series of desktop calculators. The calculator-oriented design of the 4004, as well as the very limited amount of memory which the chip could directly access (just four thousand 4-bit words), meant that no practical, general-purpose computer could be built around it. However, the first 8-bit processor from Intel, the 8008 – developed almost concurrently with the 4004 – was a different story entirely. With its 8-bit word length and more robust instruction set, the 8008 could be employed in more applications than its 4-bit predecessor. It wasn't as capable a processor as Weisbecker's FRED, but, at the time of the 8008's introduction, the FRED microprocessor existed only on the pages of RCA's technical literature.

It can easily be concluded that Kutt's APL computer wasn't a risk-free venture. With his computer expertise and status, he could easily have secured a top position with one of the North American computer manufacturers that maintained a more conservative outlook on computer use. But he decided otherwise, "because I always was more attracted to things that they said could not be done." By the end of 1971, Kutt was convinced that his computer concept was sound and realistic, and that the odds of turning it into a successful product were high. "Then," said Kutt, "you had to talk to people like Gord Ramer, who was the first big guy that I had talked into it." Soon, he would find others.

3

The Making of the MCM/70

The first months of 1972 that followed the incorporation of KSI were rather unusual. As with any typical start-up company, KSI needed capital, technology, and competent employees willing to work in an underfunded young company. What was out of the ordinary, however, was that the company's new employees were given the tasks of writing software for non-existent hardware and of building hardware out of Intel's novel semiconductor devices, whose claimed utility to the electronics industry was yet to be validated. One such device was the microprocessor. As Ramer explained, "In designing the MCM/70, we totally bet on the emerging microprocessor technology. We just proceeded, even before the first [8-bit] microprocessor was built." Another semiconductor device which Intel introduced almost concurrently with the first microprocessor was the Electrically Programmable Read-Only Memory (or EPROM).

While announcing its new devices and boldly proclaiming a "new era of integrated electronics," Intel became aware that it was in immediate need of specialized hardware and software aids to attract and support potential customers of its new memory and microprocessor products.[1] The first generation of such aids was developed by Intel's Applications Research Group during 1971 and 1972. For KSI's engineers, these microprocessor and EPROM development tools would provide a microprocessor training environment and allow them to construct the first prototype of the MCM/70. Intel's EPROM programming aids would allow Ramer and his software group to create and test the APL software for the KSI's computer. Thus the story of the design of the MCM/70 and its prototypes must begin with a brief chronicle of systems activities that took place at Intel's Applications Research Group in 1971 and early 1972.

A new era in integrated electronics

The purpose of read-only memory (ROM) in a computing device is to store programs that are needed by the device to control and monitor its operations. For instance, a ROM chip can contain the entire software of a traffic light controller or a program that boots up a standard PC, preparing all its devices to function when the PC is powered on. The content of an ordinary ROM chip is set permanently during its fabrication at a semiconductor factory. There is no direct way to correct errors or modify a program already stored in a ROM other than to manufacture a new chip with a new version of the program stored in it.

An EPROM serves the same purpose as a ROM chip. However, it can be reprogrammed many times over: its contents can be erased by exposing the device to ultraviolet light, and then reprogrammed anew using a relatively simple electronic device called an EPROM programmer. EPROMs, therefore, presented the systems engineers with cost effective alternatives to ROMs for rapid system prototyping and development. The programs destined for ROM chips could be developed and tested in-house using EPROMs, and only when an engineer was satisfied with the program (after, perhaps, several rounds of erasing and reprogramming an EPROM) was the program's code sent to a manufacturer and a non-erasable ROM chip produced.

These microprocessor and EPROM devices presented Intel with the considerable marketing challenge of reaching a wider systems engineering audience. The company's successful dissemination of its new technologies hinged upon the availability of hardware and software tools that would allow engineers to experiment with the new approach to systems design using microprocessors and EPROMs, and would permit complete in-house development of microprocessor applications.

In mid-1971, Intel's Applications Research Group under the management of Marcian E. (Ted) Hoff, Jr, the main architect of Intel's first microprocessor – the 4004 – was given the task of working closely with the marketing team to assist in promoting both the microprocessor and the EPROM. The 4004 microprocessor, originally designed as a central processing unit (or CPU) for digital desktop calculators, could be used effectively in many applications outside the confines of the calculator market. In 1971, Intel was facing a considerable marketing challenge to get this message across.

Hoff's group came to the conclusion that the best way to showcase the new devices was to use the 4004 microprocessor to execute programs stored in EPROMs. There was one technical problem, however: the 4004 was designed to work with a very specific type of ROM and was unable to communicate directly with EPROMs. In short, the 4004 required some additional interface circuitry to allow EPROMs to replace the ROMs that the 4004 CPU was designed to work with. These interface boards were designed by Applications Research engineers in mid-1971. "If I remember correctly," said Hoff, "we developed them originally for our own use. The 4004 normally worked with mask-programmed ROM, and we developed a board with an interface that allowed us to use EPROMs instead of the 4001 mask-programmed ROM."

The EPROM interface board developed by Hoff's group soon evolved into the SIM4-01 prototyping aid that used EPROMs for the development, debugging, and testing of application programs written for the 4004-based systems. The SIM4-01 was a small printed circuit board measuring 8.4 by 5.7 inches. It had sockets to hold a 4004 processor, four RAM chips (to store a total of 320 4-bit words), and four EPROMs (to store a total of 1,024 8-bit words). The board was supported with rudimentary software and design aids which were developed in-house, as well as by a select group of early Intel customers and university researchers brought together by the marketing group.

The SIM4-01 board and an inexpensive MP7-01 EPROM programmer, also developed by Hoff's engineers, caught the attention of marketing. According to Hoff, marketing originally suggested just giving the SIM4 and MP7 boards to important customers, but he opposed that idea, "feeling that we would soon want to stop such a drain on resources. Besides, we could sell them at a modest profit while our customers would find it much cheaper to pay such a price than try to develop their own version." Although intended by Intel as a program development and marketing aid to showcase Intel's new semiconductor devices, the SIM4-01 was a general purpose 4-bit computer – the first microprocessor-based computer ever designed and manufactured. In spite of its limited computing power, the SIM4 board was incorporated directly into a number of low-volume products. For instance, in 1973, Action Communication Systems of Dallas developed a high-speed dial-up communications controller in which Intel's SIM4 boards were used as front-end processors.[2]

Kutt was well aware of the microprocessor and EPROM developments at Intel. On the very day of KSI's incorporation, Hank Smith, who was in charge of Intel's Micro Computer Systems Group, signed a shipment invoice for a SIM4-01 development system, an MP7-01 EPROM programmer, and a 4004 chip set, together valued at $1,231. The shipment was destined for KSI. In spite of Hoff's objections to making the SIM4-01 a free gift to Intel's customers, Kutt's order was delivered to him at no charge. In fact, the board received by Kutt was one of the earliest versions of the SIM4, bearing the model name Intel 4004 μ-Computer.

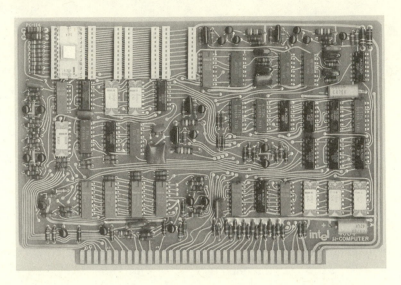

Kutt received this 4004 μ-Computer board from Intel in December 1971. (Source: York University Computer Museum, image by Z. Stachniak.)

The 4004 processor wasn't even remotely a candidate for the CPU of the MCM/70 computer. While waiting for Intel to offer its more advanced 8008 chip, however, KSI's engineers could nevertheless use the 4004 μ-Computer to experience firsthand the new microprocessor and EPROM technologies. The first hardware engineer hired by KSI was José Laraya: "The first computer that [Kutt] brought to my attention was the 4004: 'This is a computer.' And I said, 'Ya, you got to be kidding, this small chip?' But he had already been talking to Intel people. He had a good vision. And I said, 'I would be interested in working on that.'"

In April of 1972, when the first 8008 microprocessors were to come off Intel's production line, Kutt paid Intel a visit. He was accompanied by a new KSI employee, Reg Rea. "Mers knew Bob Noyce and all those guys," recollected Rea. "So he was able to get us a handful of 8008s ... It was really a neat trip. We spent two weeks in California. I just kind of followed him along since he seemed to know all these people ... We came away with a dozen or so 8008s and brought them back to Kingston."

During the trip, Kutt and Rea learned about the SIM8-01 prototyping board, a development aid analogous to the SIM4-01 but aimed at applications involving the new 8008 processor. Intel planned to introduce the 8008 microprocessor into the market in early 1972. It was only natural that the marketing strategy developed around the SIM4 and MP7 products should be adopted for the marketing of the 8008 chip. The result was the SIM8-01 microcomputer – designed, laid out, and provided with software by Hoff's Applications Research Group. "We originally designed it as a demo," remembered Hal Feeney, the main engineer working on the 8008 chip, "and we published the [SIM8-01] circuit in the early 8008 user's manual." Unlike the SIM4, the purpose of the new SIM8 board was not to resolve the problem of interfacing the microprocessor with EPROMs; the 8008 was designed to operate with standard semiconductor memories, including the EPROMs.

A month after Kutt and Rea's visit to Intel, KSI received a SIM8-01 development system and Intel's new EPROM programmer – the MP7-02 – again, at no cost to KSI. Kutt handed the SIM8-01 hardware to Laraya for evaluation and an estimation of the potential for building an APL machine around it. Regardless of the SIM8's intended application as a development and demonstration system, and not as a general-purpose computer, the board was indeed a rudimentary 8008-based microcomputer. Laraya recalled: "Mers brought it [the SIM8-01] in and said, 'Here, see what it does.' It was really computing, it really did things, one little chip."

In mid-1972, the SIM8's schematic diagram, included in the *MCS-8 User's Manual*, was the only published design of an 8-bit computer with a single-chip CPU. It was inevitable that the

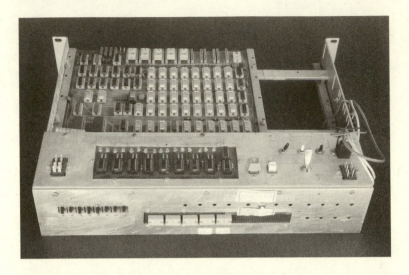

Laraya built this SIM8-01-based microcomputer in early 1972 to experiment with the Intel 8008 microprocessor and to program EPROM
devices. (Source, York University Computer Museum, photograph
courtesy of Cam Farnell.)

early design of Kutt's computer would start with a study of the
document and the testing of the SIM8-01 board. Laraya's experimentation with the SIM8-01 concentrated on interfacing it
with various devices and, later, on using the MP7-02 programmer for the purpose of moving Ramer's APL interpreter into the
EPROM chips.

The team

Following their handshake agreement in fall 1971, Kutt and
Ramer spared no effort in putting together the nucleus of KSI's
engineering and support team. The December 1971 meeting organized by Kutt and Ramer brought together the first group of
future employees, including Don Genner, José Laraya, and John
Wallace. In early 1972, that group expanded to include André
Arpin, Reg Rea, and Morgan Smyth.

Arpin would play one of the key roles in designing the memory management system for the MCM/70 computer. He came to KSI from St. Lawrence College in Kingston where, in mid-1972, Ramer assumed the directorship of the college's computer centre. Asked about his path to joining KSI, Arpin replied,

He [Ramer] talked to me and showed me the [8008] chip. And I remember bringing that thing up home. That thing had a tiny little document, right? There was nothing to it, a few pages, I don't know, maybe 30–40 pages ... it was small. And I sat down and I read the description and I just marveled at that piece of hardware. I could not believe that such a chip could exist.

Arpin, like many before him, had been indulging in pipe dreams about his own home computer for quite some time.

When I was teaching at St. Lawrence [College], I remember, I was talking to students and I said to them "in ten years from now," and that was before I even knew anything about the 8008, "in ten years from now, I will have my own computer." And the students thought that I was completely out of my skull ... And really, the year after – I had one. And when I was predicting "ten years," I thought I was optimistic. I had worked with the PDP-8 [computers before] and, in my view, I thought that the PDP-8 would be something which would get cheap enough [that, eventually,] I would be able to afford one at home.

After detailed study of the 8008's documentation, Arpin discovered one worrisome problem with the chip's design: its poor handling of the so-called interrupts, the mechanism for temporarily halting the microprocessor's operations. "I remember describing that to Gord. And we agreed: 'Well, there is a problem, but life goes on.' That's what we had, right? But otherwise, it was a marvelous chip. And Gord asked me if I was interested [in joining KSI]. And I said 'sure.'"

The design and development group at KSI was small but enthusiastic. Together they shaped and formed what would become the first personal desktop microcomputer designed specifically for individual use. Laraya and his hardware group, assisted by Rea, came up with a number of prototypes of the MCM/70 before the production model of the computer was ready. Arpin, Genner, Ramer, and Smyth created and documented the software. Reg Rea assumed the overall engineering and, later, manufacturing responsibilities. Kutt oversaw and coordinated the project, hunting for potential investors with a cardboard mock-up of the computer of the future.

In the early months of 1972, the young company operated in something of a virtual mode, with core personnel keeping their day jobs elsewhere and commuting between Ottawa, Kingston, and Toronto for meetings. KSI's first research and development lab was in the basement of Laraya's house, while the software was created on the University of Ottawa's IBM\360 computer. The company was headquartered in Kutt's house. But that was soon to change as more and more people joined KSI as full-time employees. The company's headquarters soon moved into a rented space in Willowdale, on the outskirts of Toronto. KSI's research and development facility was relocated to a rented facility in Kingston. By early 1974, MCM had twenty-six full-time employees as well as a number of part-time personnel and consultants.

From the key-cassette to the M/C prototype

Kutt's 1972 design notes disclose an urgent need to prepare a viable demonstration of the APL computer. Such demonstrations were considered vital for attracting funding and poten-

The shortcut to demo drawing. (Source: M. Kutt's archive.)

tial distributors of KSI's products. In his notes, Kutt sketches a "shortcut to demo" and estimates its completion by early June of 1972. The M/C demonstrator, as it is referred to in Kutt's notes, was to consist of a single CPU and memory board and a power supply, packed into a desktop calculator–like case featuring a built-in keyboard and a small display. It would offer basic hardware with just enough software stored in ROM to demonstrate the way the 8008 could handle a subset of APL. It is not clear whether such a minimum-hardware demonstrator was ever constructed. If it was, it would have been the work of José Laraya, who was hired to lead the hardware development of the APL computer.

José Laraya was born in the Philippines. He studied mechanical engineering at the University of the Philippines and, between 1962 and 1967, electronics engineering at Tokyo University. In 1967, he moved to Canada to work as a computer hardware engineer at Queen's University, at the very time when Kutt was the director of the Queen's computing centre. Laraya didn't work for Kutt's Consolidated Computer, but in 1971, when Kutt and Ramer were putting together the nucleus of their computer, he decided to leave Queen's for KSI, lured by Kutt's idea of building an APL computer around the Intel 8008 chip. "I had done work in semiconductors in Japan ... And I was very up to what was happening in [circuit] integration," explained Laraya. "So, I was very impressed with what Intel had done with the [8008] chip and I wanted to be one of the first to put together a [computer] processor with it." And indeed he would become one of the very first engineers to build a general-purpose computer powered by a microprocessor.

Laraya started his work on the MCM/70 computer in the first months of 1972 by experimenting with Intel's SIM8-01 prototyping system in the basement of his Kingston house. Looking back at his early experimentation with the system, Laraya recollected: "[KSI's] lab was in my basement. I had a house there [in Kingston] and I had a good set up there ... The first prototype [of the MCM/70] was on the Intel development board ... The I/O [input/output] was a teletype, the ASR-33, paper tape. So that was the first machine."[3] He recalled how tedious it was to program EPROMs with basic programs for use with this first prototype. "Those days the [EPROM] chips were very slow to program. You had to program [them] by hand, using switches." To put a code into an EPROM, one had to "set the switches and the address [on an EPROM programmer], and hit [the] 'program' [button]. And every time we programmed [a chip], Don [Genner] used to smoke one cigarette and said 'that's how long it takes to program a chip. I smoke one cigarette and when I finish – it's programmed.'"

While the educational aspect of the experiments with the SIM8-01 board was invaluable, the hardware prospects were rather discouraging. As Kutt remarks in his 1972 design notes, this early attempt at building an APL microcomputer was a disappointment. Kutt wrote that the machine "is useless as is" and had to be "drawn up, rewired, and debugged." In the end, Laraya decided to abandon the SIM8 approach and, instead, to build his own hardware from the ground up. He remembered thinking, "OK, this [SIM8-01] is fine, great, interesting, works with teletype ... But now, let's build something serious." Laraya added, "Mers got the chips and on the basis of that I developed the rack version ... It was very fast from the time we had the [SIM8-01] development board ... The software guys could play with it, we were building a computer now!"

The construction of the new prototype, which began in the basement of Laraya's house, continued in KSI's new research and development facility. "[We] decided to move just a stone's throw from my house, to ... a new but poorly constructed two-storey house," remembered Laraya. The very mention of this first KSI R&D facility, located on McKey street in Kingston next to a garbage truck repair facility, made Laraya and everybody else who worked there laugh. "That place, I'm not sure how to describe this," hesitated Arpin,

> but that place had been built by a drunk carpenter. And the floor in the building was really, really sloping, so much so that we made sure that no more than one person ever was in the middle of that room. And we used to put something like six inches of punch cards under the filing cabinets so that they did not open. [The builder] had two high-school students building that place when he was sitting in his truck drinking.

The hardware of the new prototype resided on several printed circuit boards mounted on a minicomputer-sized metal rack. "I modularized [the hardware]," recalled Laraya. "Here is the card, we will put the CPU here. I think the CPU and the display interface I put on one card. Then, there is memory. I said, 'well, these guys always want more memory,' so I put [a separate] module for EPROM and RAM." The hardware engineering team built and interfaced an APL keyboard with the computer and included a small single-line plasma display (a Burroughs

This rack of hardware is the first working prototype of the MCM/70, constructed in 1972. The "rack computer" contained three cassette tape drives on the top, a row of wire-wrapped cards below the drives, and a blue panel with a SelfScan display and switches mounted in the middle of the rack. On the bottom of the rack, there was another row of cards and the computer's power supply. (Photograph courtesy of Cam Farnell.)

Self-Scan 32-character display).[4] Soon afterward, the software group started to port a subset of APL into the prototype's EPROMs. Laraya vividly remembered some of the first computations done on the prototype.

> The first time we did a calculation [on the prototype] ...
> it took forever to crunch out the number. You could see
> it [a long computation] happening on the workspace too,
> because, at one point, we were using the display area [al-
> located in RAM] as a temporary workspace ... because we
> were so tight on RAM. You could see the numbers rolling
> up and down on the screen. And you could see, oh, that's
> about finished, because you could read the bits ... you
> could see that there was a counter decrementing and when
> you saw that the counter dropped to zero, it would flash
> the answer. So, it was fascinating to look at that small
> screen.

In his work on the rack prototype as well as on the production model of the computer, Laraya was assisted by a number of people: André Arpin, Reg Rea, Tom Moffatt, John Wallace, and others. Most architectural decisions, such as memory management, were taken in consultation with the software engineering team led by Ramer.

On 11 November 1972, the prototype was demonstrated during a special general meeting of the shareholders of Kutt Systems in Kingston, Ontario. During that meeting a motion was passed to change the name of the company to Micro Computer Machines (MCM). And finally, a name was chosen for the KSI computer: the MCM/70.

The rack prototype of the MCM/70 was soon followed by its more refined portable version. It was put on show in a special demo session during the Fifth International APL Users' Conference, which took place in Toronto in May 1973. "I remember that we had the fiberglass model there," said Laraya. "It was heating up." Ramer, too, remembered the event vividly: "The demo had to be interspersed with short talks to allow José [Laraya] to exchange the heat-sensitive parts and then restart the system for the next segment of the demo."

The demonstrated prototype already had the appearance of a remarkable computing gadget. It was small and portable. It had a built-in keyboard and a unique plasma display, and was running APL. Of course, with limited RAM and no external storage, that prototype was nothing but an advanced APL-based scientific calculator. However, although rudimentary, it did attract the attention of the APL community and made it evident that high-level programming languages such as APL would soon be readily available on small desktop machines.

The demonstration in Toronto was well attended but reactions varied. Some conference participants were clearly more impressed with IBM – which selected the conference venue to announce APL.SV, its long-awaited successor to the APL\360 language – than they were with MCM and its demonstration of a desktop APL machine. But many were astonished, like Ted Edwards, Jim Litchfield, and Glen Seeds, who left Control Data Canada to join MCM soon after the conference.

Kutt vividly remembered the reaction of one participant following the presentation: "Who are you, where did you come from?" According to Kutt, the astounded APLer was involved in the development of a personal desktop APL computer at IBM, most likely as a member of the SCAMP project (Special Computer, APL Machine Portable). SCAMP was proposed to the IBM management by Paul Friedl, an engineer in the IBM Scientific Center in Palo Alto, California, in January 1973. The project was approved later that year and given the stringent time frame of six months for the completion of the fully functional prototype. SCAMP wasn't a microcomputer; its CPU – IBM's PALM microcontroller – was not a microprocessor. "The short time available for development meant that the system had to be built from existing hardware and software components as much as possible," recollected Friedl.[5] SCAMP was never converted into a production model. Before the concept of SCAMP would re-emerge as the IBM 5100 computer late in 1975, two of the first dozen MCM/70 units manufactured by MCM in 1974 would be shipped to IBM's General Systems Division in Atlanta, Georgia, for the purpose of "research and analysis."[6] "IBM guys used to come to our press release conferences," remembered Rea. "There was always an IBM contingent there, a couple of guys, every time we had a press conference ... I would see them there and talk to them: 'What do you think about this?' just to get their feeling [about the MCM/70] – 'Well, it's kind of a toy, don't see much use for it.'" Rea acknowledged that the MCM/70's prototypes were, indeed, limited in their APL capabilities. However, continued Rea, "I was always encouraged by the fact that they were interested enough to send a couple of people."

The MCM/70 bare-bones system. (3D model of the computer courtesy of André Arpin.)

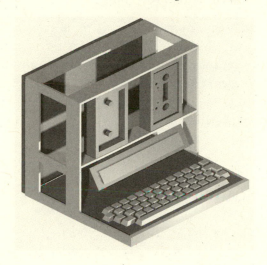

Also in early 1973, Kutt took the desktop prototype of the MCM/70 to Intel's headquarters in Santa Clara and demonstrated it to Robert Noyce and Gordon Moore, co-founders of Intel. The APL interpreter for the 8008 processor generated a lot of excitement. "They didn't believe that this little chip they were producing could do that much."[7] According to Kutt, Noyce's favorite part of the demonstration was a horse-racing game written in APL for the MCM/70 computer and its little one-line plasma display.

There were other prototypes of the MCM/70, such as a bare-bones lab version, built soon after the rack prototype. A number of these lab machines were put together and used for software development. "They were square boxes, the tape [drive mounted] on the front," recalled Arpin. "And you could carry them home. And I had one of those machines."

But one of the most successful demonstrators that the company put together had, in fact, no hardware at all. "We had a cardboard mockup of the computer," recalled Morgan Smyth. "It ... was a small, slick little box ... it was just cardboard. And we went around to a law firm in downtown Toronto and met with a bunch of senior lawyers there ... Mers was gonna try to get some venture capital." It was most likely in the office of Borden, Elliot, Kelly & Palmer, Barristers and Solicitors, where Kutt, holding the cardboard look-alike of the future MCM/70 in his hands, exclaimed, "This is what it's going to look like!" And they believed him. Kutt and Smyth left the law office with a promise of a large investment in MCM.

MCM/APL

The development of APL software for the MCM/70 computer was the most challenging aspect of the personal computer project at MCM. After all, the success of the future MCM/70 in the marketplace would depend not so much on its novel hardware makeup, which might excite the technical press, as on how useful and user-friendly it would become. And that meant writing quality software for a microprocessor characterized by low speed and a restricted set of instructions. That also meant compressing APL into a useful dialect which, when implemented, could fit into the limited memory space of the computer. "The fact that we were able to do this," commented Glen Seeds, who joined MCM in June 1973, "led directly to the name of our implementation [of the APL language]. IBM's version was officially titled 'APL\360', and was intended to be read as 'APL expands the (IBM) 360 (system).' APLers will recognize this as a pun on the 'expand' operator '\'. Taking our cue from this, we called ours 'MCM/APL', to be read as 'MCM compresses APL'."[8]

The work on the APL language for the MCM/70 began in early 1972, when KSI was still waiting for Intel to make the 8008 chip and its documentation available to the electronics industry, and months before the final hardware architecture of the MCM/70 was drawn up. The team that was developing the APL language – Ramer, Genner, and Smyth – had worked together

Morgan Smyth (left), Don Genner, André Arpin, and Gordon Ramer (right) at York University, Toronto, 2001. (Source: York University Computer Museum, photograph by Z. Stachniak.)

before. Ramer implemented his York APL with the assistance of Genner, who also worked at York University Computer Centre. Smyth was among the first users of the York APL and he frequently commuted between his workplace – then called Ryerson Polytechnic Institute in Toronto – and York University to discuss the implementation issues of York APL with Ramer and Genner. At MCM, the trio would develop one of the first high-level programming languages for a microprocessor: Ramer would design it, Genner would help with its implementation, and Smyth would document it in the excellent MCM/70 *User's Guide*, published by MCM in 1974.

But how does one develop an APL language for a computer that does not exist, even on paper? To answer this question, Laraya pointed out that "they [Ramer and Genner] knew it would be an 8-bit computer and they were fascinated by the fact that it would run on this 8-bit single chip." Having only the specifications of the general architecture of the 8008 processor and its instruction set – that is, the list of operations that the microprocessor could perform – Ramer and Genner used the assembler language for the IBM\360 computer to emulate the operations of the 8008 chip. In other words, they replicated the functionality of the 8008 chip on a mainframe computer. "So, that way," continued Laraya, "they could write the [MCM/APL] code without having the actual machine."

Ramer and Genner used an APL terminal located at St. Lawrence College in Kingston and remotely connected to an IBM computer at the University of Ottawa to do all the initial work on MCM/APL. When the rack prototype of the microcomputer was finally working in mid-1972 at MCM's research and development facility in Kingston, the software development could be done directly on the 8008-based hardware and the MCM/APL code could be transferred into EPROMs using Intel's MP7 programmer.

In his notes, Kutt briefly sketches KSI's directions for the development of the APL language for the MCM/70 microcomputer. First, the basic, stripped-down version of APL\360 would be implemented. He notes that such a restricted version would be particularly useful for demonstrations of early prototypes of the computer which likely would operate with a very limited memory. Then the basic version of the language was to be extended in two directions to support the scientific as well as the business use of the MCM/70.

In the end, Ramer's team created a single dialect of the APL\360 language. Apart from APL functions, it supported a limited but direct communication with the computer, making its use more flexible and user friendly. "When we came up with the APL [language] for our PC," commented Kutt, "our prime target was to make it simple to use ... so the user wouldn't have to become embroiled in the little nitty-gritty things you have to look after in APL."

The full description of MCM/APL appeared in the *MCM/70 User's Guide*. In the guide, as well as in the MCM promotional literature, MCM/APL was declared a powerful and natural small-system language, easy to learn and easy to use. "You will find that, after only a brief exposure to the [APL] language and to the MCM/70, you will be performing computer applications which normally take you weeks to do with any other language."[9] The 270-page guide, authored by Smyth, is a well-written early document on the general architecture, functionality, and programming of one of the first microcomputers.

When Ramer agreed to lead the software development for the MCM/70 computer, he understood quite well that his success would hinge upon the hardware engineers finding some creative way to substantially extend the 16K of memory that the 8008 chip was designed to operate with directly. The first solution to the memory problem Laraya and his group adopted was to divide the computer's ROM into the core portion of 6K and a number of 2K blocks, called banks. The core portion of ROM contained the minimum software necessary to operate the computer at any given time. The banks, on the other hand, contained separate pieces of software that could be accessed individually and only when needed. This technique, known as bank switching, allowed MCM to store its software first in 14K of ROM memory and later, with an improved version of APL, in 22K of ROM.

Bank switching took care of one memory problem only: creating enough ROM space to store MCM/APL. The execution of an APL program on an MCM/70 was another issue altogether. A user's application program and its input data together required additional memory for their storage. This is what computer random access memory (RAM) is for. Clearly, the size of RAM delimits the size of programs and the amount of input data that can be processed. Both APL\360 and York APL allocated 32K of memory for that purpose (the so-called APL workspace) to each APL user. This was much more than the 8008 could handle directly; the chip could address only 16K of memory, 6K of which was already allocated for the core portion of ROM. That left the MCM engineers with no more than 10K of APL workspace, which was insufficient for all but the most trivial applications.

To solve this "RAM shortage" problem, MCM built a virtual memory system into the MCM/70. Briefly, a virtual memory system uses external storage to extend its RAM capacity. When the execution of a program requires more RAM than is currently available, some part of the RAM that contains information not vital to the current state of the program's execution is copied into the external storage, freeing enough RAM space to complete the computation. The relocated information is brought back from the external storage to RAM when needed. Virtual memory on MCM's computer was a matter of necessity. Without it, there would be no APL on the MCM/70; most of the memory of the little computer would be consumed to store a program and input data, and very little (if any) would be left for the program's execution.

"Virtual memory was mine," said Arpin. "There were a number of things that were obvious. Like ... we had to be able to save the workspace. And it became obvious when we worked with the [prototype of the] machine that it was too small." In the 1960s Arpin was developing software for Canada Life Insurance Company "that took advantage of loading programs in and out and actually loaded data in and out as well. So it was obvious to me," continued Arpin, "that you could do that [for the MCM/70]." What André Arpin and José Laraya came up with was the implementation of virtual memory using a specially designed digital cassette drive as external storage. Looking back at the adopted solution for virtual memory, Arpin commented that "doing that on a digital tape, on a cassette

André Arpin explaining the MCM/70's virtual memory at York University in 2003. (Source: York University Computer Museum, photograph by Z. Stachniak.)

tape, seemed like insanity, but it was actually not that bad, it actually worked. People used that for doing some pretty serious programming and quite successfully."

The MCM/70's virtual memory operated under the AVS software (A Virtual System) written by Arpin. The user had the option of operating the MCM/70 in either the virtual or non-virtual mode. When AVS was activated (virtual mode), both the computer's RAM and the unused space on the cassette tape became the user's workspace. With virtual memory implemented, the MCM/70 offered in excess of 100K of memory, an astonishing amount for such a small system. Commenting on the virtual memory solution for the MCM/70, Arpin noted that "if you were willing to live with the [low] speed of the machine, you could do some incredible things." He recalled that an MCM/70 was used to run simulations for the Pickering nuclear plant on the north shore of Lake Ontario.

They ran simulations on it and they were quite successful. ... They used to rent the [computing] time on I.P. Sharp [Associates' time-sharing system] before that. It cost them a fortune. They were able to move their code over [to their MCM/70]. They had to adjust it but ... it wasn't that drastic an adjustment. It [MCM/70] ran slow ... [but] they only had to run it once a day. So, those people who were spending, I think, hundreds of dollars an hour on the [I.P. Sharp Associates] computer, were suddenly paying 5,000 dollars for the machine that would do that [simulation]; and they would recover the costs extremely quickly.

The computers used by commercial time-sharing companies, such as I.P. Sharp Associates of Toronto, were, of course, much larger and much faster than the MCM/70. But the response time of these computers, which sat in air-conditioned computer rooms, depended on the number of users remotely connected to them at any given time. Unless a user was prepared to connect to a time-sharing system outside normal business hours, the MCM/70 was actually more cost-effective for typical business tasks. It allowed continuous, twenty-four-hour-a-day access to computing resources at fixed computing costs. In comparison with a time-sharing system, an MCM/70's use did not require signing on, dialling a telephone, or entering an account number. Its dedicated use didn't require communications links, and hence wasn't affected by line-noise and line-drops which, for users of time-sharing systems, could wreck their computer sessions. MCM/70 users could develop and run dedicated software, and they could afford to take breaks as there was no need to hurry through terminal sessions to do as much work per connect hour as possible to save costs.

The MCM/70's ROM contained not only the APL language interpreter but also its operating system, comprised of AVS and EASY (which stands for External Allocation SYstem). The

MCM/70's operating system provided the user with a conven-
ient way to store, retrieve, and delete data and user-defined
functions from the computer's cassette. Not even as capable as
the first versions of Microsoft Windows, the MCM/70's operating system nevertheless had certain novel features that did
not appear in other operating systems for PCs until the late
1980s. One such feature was the computer's ability to be turned
off with an operating system command rather than with a
physical switch. Glenn Seeds commented on this feature of the
MCM/70's operating system: "The one thing that seemed obvious to us that no one else thought of ... was not having an off
switch, but powering down with an OS [operating system] command, to ensure protection of your data ... Even today, the use
of automatic UPS-supported shutdown, with resume on restart,
is uncommon."[10] Indeed, an on/off switch was nowhere to be
found on the production model of MCM's computer. To start it,
the user had only to press the START key and the computer responded with "MCM/APL" on the screen to indicate that it was
ready for use. To switch the computer off, one typed "□OFF"
and pressed the RETURN key. Before the computer could be
deactivated, the entire contents of the workspace and its status
were preserved on the cassette.

> This is to ensure that nothing is accidentally destroyed. In
> order to have the system restore them [the workspace and
> its status] back in the computer at some later date, the cas-
> sette must be mounted in the tape drive before the START
> key is pressed. If this is done, the computer will automatic-
> ally reconstruct the saved items in memory to appear as
> though the □OFF function had never been executed.[11]

The APL/EASY/AVS software on the MCM/70 made the
MCM/70 a micro-mainframe. In 1972, APL was installed exclusively on mainframe computers. Virtual memory was available only on mainframe computers such as the IBM System\370

Models 158 and 168 – one of the first lines of mainframes to operate with virtual memory.

The production model of the MCM/70

The work on the MCM/70 was finished in 1974 and was a remarkable achievement of both the software and the hardware engineers at MCM. The computer was small and portable, and operated under sophisticated APL/AVS/EASY software. The computer was packaged in a well-designed case that resembled future popular personal computers such as Apple][, introduced by Apple Computer in 1977, or the Atari 800 released by Atari Corporation the following year. The MCM/70's built-in keyboard was well-designed and provided both alphanumeric and special APL characters.

Although the little plasma display screen could only display thirty-two characters at any given time, a user could enter up to eighty-five characters to form a single line of input. In cases where the number of characters typed exceeded the thirty-two-character limit, the computer would automatically shift all the characters it was currently displaying one position to the left as each additional character was entered. A user could use the "arrow keys" of the keyboard to scroll left, right, up, and down to view all the characters entered on possibly multiple lines.

In other ways, the computer was like a digital calculator, as envisioned by Kutt. Without any knowledge of computer hardware, installation procedures, or machine language programming, a novice computer user could operate an MCM/70 and execute simple programs almost instantly. One just had to plug the computer into a power outlet and press the START key. When the little screen displayed the "MCM/APL" prompt, one could type (3×4)+6 and the computer would respond with 18 on the screen. Of course, more advanced applications required a detailed study of MCM/APL and the MCM/70's operating system.

This MCM/70 computer is one of the first production models manufactured by MCM at its Kingston plant. It was used for internal applications at MCM. (Source: York University Computer Museum,
photograph by Paul Stachniak.)

The MCM/70 was also designed to work with peripherals. It
could drive a printer and later, with the introduction of the improved model /700 in 1975, a range of other peripherals such as
external displays (the VDU-2480 and VDU-9620), floppy-disk
drive systems (the SDS-250 and DDS-500), a punch card reader
(the PMR-400), and a modem (for models equipped with the
SCI-1200 Communications subsystem). The MCM/700 could
have as much as 32K of ROM (containing EASY, AVS, and an
improved MCM/APL language) and could use one of the disk-
drive systems for virtual memory, due to some clever design decisions made by André Arpin when he was still working on the

original cassette version of AVS. Arpin described this, modestly, as a coincidence. "When people switched from tape to disk, it was absolutely compatible, their code would just work on a disk. I didn't foresee that ... but this [design] was just a marvelous solution that we came to, it just worked so well when we went to disk."

The original design of the MCM/70 also called for a power failure protection system. It was a subsystem of the computer's power supply that allowed continuous operation by battery in the event of power failure. For extended power loss, the computer initiated an orderly shutdown: it automatically provided a system back-up by copying the content of RAM to a cassette before shutdown. The system was automatically reinstated when power was restored and batteries were recharged. Unfortunately, the engineering problems with this type of power failure protection system unnecessarily delayed the introduction of the MCM/70 to the market.

The work on the MCM/70's prototypes had culminated with the first official showing of the computer in May 1973 during the APL conference in Toronto. MCM used the conference venue to make it official: small but powerful personal computers were coming and MCM was going to make them. To make its message loud and clear, the company would spend the rest of the year extensively promoting its APL computer across North America and Europe.

4

Unveiling the Future

The computer industry at large was mostly unaware of the developments at MCM. The company kept most of its secrets well guarded, only occasionally releasing information to the press. Although some vague press reports talked about Kutt's plans to set up a new computer company,[1] it was not until March 1973 that a short note in *Canadian Datasystems* informed readers about the coming of a "small computer" from a new Canadian firm:

> After keeping a low profile for 18 months, Kutt has acquired space in suburban Toronto and formed Micro Computer Machines Ltd ... The company, he [Kutt] says, is looking at the very small computer market, using advanced LSI [large scale integration] technology ... Kutt described the project as "pretty exciting," but said it would be inappropriate to release information, until full specifics are available ... To date, no products have been released but Kutt says a couple of major announcements will be made within two months.[2]

Five months had passed and there was still no official announcement of the MCM/70 in Canada, not even a press conference – only a limited demonstration to the APL community in May, and a few hints that made the mystery of the esoteric new hardware from MCM even more alluring:

MERS KUTT IS BACK WITH MINICOMPUTERS

New technology is behind a range of minicomputers to be announced, probably next month, by Micro Computer Machines Ltd, Toronto ... Kutt is tight-lipped on specifics, but told CD [*Canadian Datasystems*] the computers are extremely small and will have a "dramatic impact" on the market. High-density chips and circuits are said to make them unlike anything now available.[3]

While readers of *Canadian Datasystems* were puzzling over the phrase "'dramatic impact' on the market," the prototype of the MCM/70 was on its European tour, which began with the APL Congress held in Copenhagen, Denmark, 22 to 24 August. The Copenhagen event was the largest gathering of APL researchers and practitioners in 1973 and an invaluable opportunity for MCM to showcase its APL computer.

MCM's demonstration was indeed unique; the MCM/70 arrived from Canada in an attaché case. This unusual packaging was not meant to protect the computer from possible damage during the trip; it was the computer's actual case, housing all the MCM/70's hardware and the Ni-Cd batteries that powered this crude laptop. In short, MCM was bringing to Copenhagen a small, luggable, APL computer – the first microcomputer in a briefcase. "Ted did carry the briefcase model onto the plane," recollected Glen Seeds. "Can you imagine trying to get a lash-up prototype in a briefcase containing electronic devices connected to several heavy 1½ inch by 3 inch cylinders past airport security today?!" But it was not passing through airport security with the first laptop that should be recorded as a landmark in computing history, but the first in-flight operation of such a device. "Ted used it on the plane to work on the presentation he was delivering in Copenhagen," added Seeds.

The man who brought the MCM/70 to Copenhagen was Ted Edwards. A glance through the congress proceedings reveals that Edwards wrote his APL paper for presentation at the congress as an employee of Control Data Canada (CDC).[4] However, by the time the conference proceedings were printed, Edwards had left CDC to join MCM. Almost thirty years later, Edwards described his move to MCM as a rather unusual professional opportunity:

> I moved to Toronto in 1970 to take a position with Control Data Canada in charge of developing an APL interpreter for the CDC STAR, then the world's "largest" computer. By Spring of 1973, APL*STAR was up and running and documented, ready for release. Unfortunately, it was the only STAR software that was. Rather than go to work on COBOL (fate worse that death for an APLer), I and two of my guys, Jim Litchfield and Glen Seeds, left CDC to go to MCM. After all, after doing an APL for the world's largest computer, what was one to do other than an APL for the world's smallest, the Intel 8008?[5]

According to Edwards, it was his idea to pack an MCM/70 into an attaché case. "I was already committed to deliver a paper at the 1973 Copenhagen APL conference when I joined MCM and had the idea of building a machine into an attaché case with some batteries. I figured that it would certainly attract some attention and indeed, it did."

As was the case with the MCM's main product, the making of the computer-in-a-briefcase, or the MCM/70 Executive as it was later called, was a team effort. "We all worked on it and we all stayed up late trying to get him [Edwards] on the plane," said Laraya. "We got a Grand & Toy briefcase, just the right size.

Edwards demonstrates the MCM/70 Executive during the 1973 APL Congress in Copenhagen. (Source: "Computer i en kuffert," *Politiken*, 23 August 1973.)

It was very difficult to stick it [the hardware] into that briefcase." The portable computer had a flat aluminum top panel with the keyboard on the bottom and the digital cassette drive and plasma display occupying the top left and top right of the panel, respectively.

Edwards demonstrated the MCM/70 Executive to the attendees of the Congress on the very first day. The computer attracted the attention of not only the APLers gathered at the Congress but also of the Danish daily *Politiken*, which on 23 August reported enthusiastically about the presentation in a front page article "Computer i en kuffert," giving a detailed description of the "revolutionary computer." The photographs taken for the *Politiken* article depicted Edwards operating the MCM/70 on the Technical University of Denmark's campus where the APL congress was taking place.

But it was Kutt who skillfully exploited the *Politiken* article to give the MCM computer wide European exposure, arranging press conferences, interviews, and trade presentations in France, Germany, Holland, Italy, Switzerland, and the United Kingdom, including the unveiling of the MCM/70 at the Canadian High Commission in London on 10 September. He arrived in Europe in late August with a desktop prototype of the MCM/70. "From that [exposure in *Politiken*]," recollected Kutt, "I was able to use trade commissioners in different countries that I was going to visit to really juice up press conferences. We had great turnouts at the press conferences."

Every major stop on MCM's European tour was an occasion for Kutt to paint his vision of future computing – of millions of inexpensive computers powered by the microprocessor – and to boldly proclaim that it was his MCM/70 that might "revolutionize the world of computers in the same way that pocket calculators revolutionized the world of calculators." The media followed suit, praising the sensational new computer from Canada as one that would be setting standards in the computer industry for years to come.[6]

France was the final leg of the tour. In Paris, Kutt went through what had become his usual routine of pre-arranged interviews, including a guest appearance on a technology program broadcast by French national television. From the history of technology point of view, however, it is MCM's participation in the SICOB'73 exhibit, more than the interviews, that deserves attention.

The SICOB'73 exhibit (Salon de l'informatique, de la communication et de l'organisation du bureau) took place in Paris from 19 to 28 September. SICOB was one of the main European computer and information technology shows, and MCM hoped to attract the attention of the computer industry to the new computing paradigm represented by its product. While this did not happen – the small computer from MCM was largely ignored by the technology observers – Kutt could see for the first time that, in the microcomputer business, MCM was no longer alone. There was a French competitor, a small electronics systems house called Réalisations et Études Électroniques (R2E).

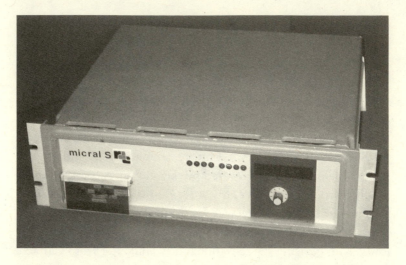

R2E's second generation computer, the Micral S, utilized the Intel 8080 microprocessor. (Courtesy of Association pour un conservatoire de l'informatique et de la télématique (ACONIT), Grenoble, France, photograph by Z. Stachniak.)

During the SICOB show, R2E presented its own 8008-based microcomputer, the Micral.

Before we enter the SICOB'73 exhibit area in search of the MCM/70 and the Micral, we should back up and examine the Micral's origins. The corporate histories of MCM and R2E have many parallels. Both companies were 1971 startups, brought to life by gifted entrepreneurs. Both introduced early microprocessor-based products aimed at markets in which the use of minicomputers was unnecessarily expensive, complex, and inflexible.

R2E was founded by Vietnam-born engineer (André) Thi T. Truong around the same time as Kutt was incorporating KSI. In early 1972, Truong, like Kutt, was touring Silicon Valley in search of electronics novelties. He returned with the 8008 microprocessor. In mid-1972 the Institute Nationale de la Recherche Agronomique (INRA), the French National Agricultural

Research Institute, contracted R2E to develop an inexpensive, mobile, and programmable process control system that could reliably handle a large number of peripherals. The solution proposed by R2E was an 8008-based computer that the company called the Micral. The detailed architecture of the computer was the work of François Gernelle. In his work on the Micral, Gernelle was assisted by a number of people including B. Chetrite, M. Benchetrit, M. Joubert, G. Lledo, and A. Rainaud.

The Micral was announced in Paris in February of 1973.[7] The INRA project moved R2E up to the front line of pioneering work on microprocessor-based computers. In contrast to the MCM/70, R2E's computer was designed not as a personal computer but as a microprocessor-based digital control system. Although the Micral's hardware architecture was well designed and allowed for easy upgrades of the computer in the future, its basic configuration was not impressive. The computer, soon renamed the Micral N (for "Normal"), initially came with only 256 bytes of RAM and could only be programmed using machine language instructions composed of zeros and ones. To enter a program into the computer, the user had to laboriously set the toggle switches located on the front panel of the computer. Every byte of information required setting eight switches, one per bit.

The Micral N was not a personal computer and was clearly unable to do any of the tasks the MCM/70 was designed for. But the production of the MCM/70 would not commence until 1974, whereas by the end of 1973, R2E had already sold five hundred of its microcomputers, making R2E the first manufacturer of volume-produced, fully assembled microcomputers, and giving the Micral the title of the earliest commercially sold, fully assembled and supported microcomputer.

The Micral made its debut on the American scene in May of 1974 during the National Computer Conference in Chicago. R2E showed the prototype of its advanced version of the

R2E's "you don't need a hammer to crush a fly" advertising brochure, National Computer Conference in Chicago, 1974. (Source: York University Computer Museum.)

Micral – the Micral S ("Super") – built around Intel's new and more sophisticated processor, the 8080. The software library included, among other products, the programming language BAL ("Business Application Language," also called "Business-Oriented BASIC Language") written by Michel Joubert, who was in charge of the R2E's software development. The computer was designed to operate with a variety of peripherals: cathode-ray tube (CRT) displays, printers, cassette recorders, modems, card and paper tape readers and punches, and magnetic disk and tape storage devices. The R2E's Micral S was shown in Chicago with a keyboard and CRT display.

Truong argued that the computational needs of customers in a vast number of areas would be better served, not by wired logic systems or minicomputers, but by microprocessor-based systems. He considered R2E Micrals, and microcomputers in general, a cost-effective alternative to minicomputers in applications that did not require the full computing power of a mini. "You don't need a hammer to crush a fly," reads the headline on the Micral advertising brochure distributed by R2E during the 1974 National Computer Conference in Chicago. "You wouldn't use the hammer to crush a fly just as you wouldn't take a minicomputer to compute a small process." With the analogy established, R2E proclaimed,

> To crush a fly, a fly swatter is surely more efficient than a
> hammer. As complete but not as fast ... Micral is surely
> more efficient than a minicomputer in a lot of real-time
> applications: process control, teletransmission, scientific
> instrumentation, teaching, etc. Micral is the link between
> wired circuitry and minicomputers.

However, the American market turned out to be much more difficult to penetrate than the European. While the Micral's technical features and its modest price of $1,950 (for the basic configuration) generated 1,000 orders by the end of 1974 from European industrial and business customers, in the United States R2E's line of Micral computers was largely ignored by industry as well as by the technical and trade press. The situation did not improve even after the Micral S was licensed to Warner & Swasey, Electronic Product Division, of Solon, Ohio.[8] It was not until June of 1976 that the Warner & Swasey Micral Microcomputer System ($12,000 for the WS Micral in basic configuration) was shown in the United States during the National Computer Conference in New York. By that time the technological novelty represented by the Micral, as well as the price advantage, was all but lost.

Returning to the SICOB 1973 exhibit in Paris: the MCM/70 and the Micral did not go entirely unnoticed by the technology observers, but the exhibition floor really belonged to other small computer systems and programmable desktop calculators offered by Digital Equipment, Hewlett-Packard, Wang Laboratories, and German manufacturer Diehl Datensystem. What did go unnoticed at SICOB, despite Kutt's and Truong's best efforts, was the harbinger of a dramatic shift in the computer industry soon to be brought about by microprocessor-powered computers such as the MCM/70 and the Micral. R2E and MCM products were aimed at distinct markets which already represented two major application areas for future computers; the Micral represented inexpensive controllers and embedded computer systems, and the MCM/70 was the forerunner of a versatile personal computer.

Kutt understood well that to sell novel hardware, a company needs to promote a killer application. But at SICOB, he could only offer MCM/APL and the Horse Race game. Perhaps there were visitors who tried to do an ad hoc APL calculation on the displayed MCM/70. But many more SICOB attendees descended on Digital Equipment's booth, mesmerized by the moon-landing simulation that ran on DEC's PDP-11/45 system. As one visitor recollected, "One could control, by means of a 'light pen' acting on the screen, the thrust and orientation of one's space-ship, while the machine kept track of the residual fuel, and displayed your position and orientation relative to a rugged landscape."[9]

Remember that in the fall of 1973, the Micral N had just started to ship, the MCM/70 existed only as a prototype, and the world of electronics was still under the spell of desktop and pocket calculators. Some of these calculators, such as Hewlett-Packard's 9830, could even execute simple BASIC programs, which was seen as a major step forward. It was not until years later that people realized that these programmable calculators could be replaced by general purpose microcomputers.

The veil of secrecy about MCM and its microcomputer was finally lifted in North America at the end of the MCM/70's European tour. The MCM computer was officially announced

The announcement of the MCM/70 in Toronto. From left: Mers Kutt, Gordon Ramer, Ted Edwards, and Reg Rea, with a prototype of the MCM/70. (Source: York University Computer Museum, photographer unknown.)

in Toronto on 25 September at a press conference in the Royal York Hotel, then in New York on the 27th, and in Boston on the 28th. Extensive North American press coverage followed.[10] In New York, Kutt told reporters and technology observers that "the trend in the computer field toward usage of more small computers and a limited number of large computers, could result in the MCM/70 in a few years becoming 'as familiar as calculators are today.'"[11]

There are only a few known photographs from these early press conferences. One published by *The Toronto Star* two days after the 25 September press conference, showed Mers Kutt assisting Edwards' twelve-year-old daughter Kim to operate the computer. At the time, marketing of computer technology frequently employed a youthful theme, such as a child playing with the keyboard of a computer. Clearly, young children could not possibly operate mainframe or minicomputers of the 1960s and early 1970s; such ads were designed only to stop a reader from turning a page and to focus on the message conveyed by them.

An early MCM promotional brochure depicting a prototype of the MCM/70, 1973. (Source: York University Computer Museum.)

On the other hand, children found operating microcomputers easy and fascinating – especially those little home computers that would start to appear on the consumer market at the end of the 1970s and early 1980s.

The message delivered during the press conferences was simple but powerful. MCM intended to make the world's first portable APL computer "of a size, price and ease-of-use as to bring personal computer ownership to business, education and scientific users previously unserved by the computer industry."[12] MCM's promotional brochures explained that the MCM/70 would

> bridge the gap between the sophisticated calculators that offer simplicity of operation but fail to provide the information processing capabilities of the computer ... and the large and complex mainframe computers that require such high degrees of training and experience as to place them beyond the operational capabilities of most people who want to use them.[13]

For business and scientific use, the MCM/70 offered a low-cost APL programming environment. For educational purposes, MCM promised the 'MCM/70 Classroom' – an environment that would provide each student with his or her own individualized interactive computer. MCM recognized that in the early 1970s, one of the main obstacles to advancing the use of computers in education was the high cost of computer equipment. According to MCM, the most effective system would be one which allowed each student to use a separate terminal to enter into direct and interactive communication with the computer. MCM estimated that the use of the MCM/70s as stand-alone terminals could reduce computing costs to just 25¢ per student hour versus the $25 cost of a typical academic terminal-based time-sharing system.

In his early analysis of the academic market, Kutt looked primarily at the IBM System\360 users, who might benefit from the smaller and much cheaper APL system. He estimated that there were about fifteen prospective universities in Canada and seventy-five in the United States. To attract them to its products, MCM developed special educational presentations. One of these, delivered by Edwards in October at the University of Toronto as part of the university's "Small Computer Seminars," brought a record turnout of 115 people and, according to the organizers, was an outstanding success. Some university professors wrote to MCM expressing their direct interest in the MCM hardware: "APL is currently used in all of our introductory courses so that the potential for systems like yours at Yale is very high," wrote Martin H. Schultz, Professor of Computer Science at Yale University, in November 1973. By 1976, an estimated 27.5 per cent of the MCM systems sold in North America went to educational institutions.

Before the year's end, the MCM/70 was displayed at one more computer show. The Canadian Computer Show & Conference (CCSC) was organized for the first time in 1969 by the Canadian Information Processing Society under the presidency of Mers Kutt himself. In 1973, the combined computer show and conference took place in Toronto from 16 to 18 October, and was already Canada's premier computer event. "Among new exhibitors [at CCSC] will be an old face," reported *The Financial Post* on 29 September, "that of Mers Kutt, ex-president of Consolidated Computers Ltd, whose new company, Micro Computer Machines Inc., will be showing a Kutt-invented world first: a complete battery-operated computer-in-a-briefcase, with cassette storage." In fact, at CCSC, MCM would exhibit two models of the MCM/70: the desktop and the Executive versions. The MCM products attracted steady attention throughout the exhibition period at CCSC. It was gratifying for Kutt to read reviews in post-show commentaries of not only the MCM/70 but also of two new key-edit systems exhibited by his former company, Consolidated Computer.

The announcement in Toronto of two machines – the typewriter-sized desktop computer and the battery-operated MCM/70 Executive – was a typical example of how MCM would continue trying to develop too many products with insufficient financial and human resources. According to Laraya, two briefcase MCM/70 prototypes were constructed, but the company had never converted them into production models. Fortunately, added Laraya, MCM started questioning the validity of the briefcase model as a product when the desktop version was yet to be manufactured. "It was OK to demonstrate it but to make it, to fashion it out of the briefcase: what about your venting? We were shoehorning everything in … it was tough to do it."

At the close of 1973, MCM was in an excellent position to build and successfully market its PC. The MCM/70 was shown throughout North America and Europe, and recognized as a breakthrough in the computer industry. The company had sufficient engineering and marketing expertise to convert the MCM/70 prototype into a production model and to negotiate successful agreements with prospective North American distributors for its computer products. MCM was fully aware of the new era in computing that microprocessor technology was about to usher in and wanted to play the main role in its launch.

5

It's All About Power

1973 was a successful year for MCM, one in which the company made excellent progress in both product development and marketing. By the end of the year, the company had engaged most of its resources in the process of converting the prototype into the production model, and it seemed for a while that the mass manufacture of the computer would commence with the dawning of 1974. The production targets were estimated at an astonishing level of 500 to 1,000 machines a month, which would generate enough cash not only to satisfy the most profit-hungry investors but also to develop the next generation of MCM computers.

Although some MCM/70 units manufactured in-house were indeed shipped to distributors in early 1974, and the pilot run and shipments continued through the year, the launch of full-scale production was disrupted by a prolonged and devastating power struggle between Kutt and some of MCM's investors. The corporate unrest culminated in October 1974: Mers Kutt was forced out of the company which, by then, was barely showing signs of life.

From the history of computing's point of view, the events at MCM in 1974 provide a unique opportunity to identify the technological and corporate challenges faced by companies on the front line of personal computing in jump-starting the new industry. These pioneers paid dearly for being there first, but being unable to raise their corporate banners high enough to lead the pack. The MCM/70 started shipping in 1974 but did not sell in the thousands, as the company had hoped. Its cleaned-up version, the MCM/700, actually sold well in 1975 and created a fair-sized market niche for personal APL computers, especially within the education, insurance, and actuarial markets. But when the dust finally settled on the desks of those at MCM who survived the stormy days of 1974, the company was stripped of its enthusiasm and corporate innocence. It was left without technology champions and visionaries. The new and vibrant personal computer industry that MCM helped to develop would end up pushing MCM to its fringes, where the company would struggle for survival until its end in 1982.

This book will not provide unequivocal conclusions that explain what went wrong with a company that in 1973 was flying high, with a magnificent product praised throughout North America and Europe for boldly challenging the established frontiers of computing. To the disappointed reader, it can only offer a possible interpretation of crucial events, pieced together from facts and recollections, frequently inconsistent, incomplete, and distorted by time, and recalled with difficulty and emotion by those who directly participated in them. And so, we begin.

Too much with too little?

The enthusiasm streaming from the events of 1973 induced the company to set its corporate objectives very high. MCM's internal document, *Development Policy*, authored by Ramer and marked "Confidential," defined them as follows:

• to place MCM in a financial position allowing the
  Company to explore new technologies, evaluate
  alternatives, and produce products of excellent quality and
  integrity, to the best of its abilities;

- to achieve and maintain a position of leadership in the
  APL community;
- to maintain a posture which allows the Company to
  implement new technologies, minimizing time and effort
  to accomplish this.

For MCM, still in a start-up position, a simple and sound business strategy which was consistent with these objectives would have been to promptly develop the production model of the MCM/70 and to direct a portion of profits derived from the sales of the computer to finance the company's research and development activities. Although the MCM/70 had always been the main product under development and its Executive model – the computer-in-a-briefcase – was terminated as soon as the big computer shows of 1973 were over, MCM was beginning to lose its focus. In addition to the MCM/70, MCM launched concurrent hardware projects and initiatives that tied up the company's personnel and resources. In the first months of 1974, MCM was spending $60,000 a month on average, an amount which was unsustainable unless cash started to flow in from sales of the computers. In addition to the MCM/70, the company wanted to develop the MCM/70T intelligent terminal, the MCM/170 small business system, and a new model of the MCM/70 based on the most recent microprocessor from Intel, the 8080. The hardware configuration of the MCM/70 itself was undergoing continuous upgrades: its power supply was evolving into a state-of-the-art device, and the company also initiated several interface projects aimed at connecting the MCM/70 to a range of peripherals, from printers and plotters to CRT displays, card readers, and modems. Furthermore, the company was engaged in the development or adaptation of peripherals for its computers, such as a printer station with built-in numeric keypad and audio-cassette storage.

Looking back at that critical moment in MCM's history, André Arpin said that to succeed with its MCM/70 product, the company should have adopted and followed rather obvious product development directives "to have very clear and well defined targets and [to] stop on these targets. Don't make them move. Freeze them and say: this is all we're going to do and until this is done we are not going to do anything else. If we cannot sell this product at that point, we fail. Adding bells and whistles to it, if nobody is interested, doesn't get you anywhere." While some of these additional projects were justified (the MCM/70 had to be able to work at least with a printer, and plans had to be made for the next generation of MCM computers), other initiatives, such as plans for protecting the MCM/70 from third-party plug-in peripherals, could have been rescheduled or contracted out, or had their rationale re-evaluated.

The case that perhaps best illustrates how MCM's business strategy lost its focus is the contract which MCM signed with the TCF company in mid-1973. According to that contract, worth $35,000 in seed money, MCM was to develop a small but complete computer business system comprised of the TCF computer (referred to as the MCM/170 in MCM's internal documents), a display, and a printer, as well as floppy disk and cassette storage systems. At first, the TCF contract was seen as an opportunity to develop an MCM computer business system around the MCM/70 without much effort. However, in the first months of 1974, it become evident that the MCM/170 could not possibly emerge from the MCM/70 hardware.

In March 1974, Michael R. Day, MCM's manager of operations, made a significant effort to properly assess the company's prospects regarding the TCF contract. The result of his study, distributed to management personnel as a memo entitled *Why we should abandon the TCF project*, was a critical look at both the TCF project and the company's overall business plan. "From the first, I have been skeptical of our ability to complete the [TCF] contract while at the same time pursuing our MCM/70," began Day. "Now, ten months and minimal progress later, I see no reason for changing my mind."

In Day's opinion, MCM viewed the TCF system as the company's possible entry into the lucrative small business computer market. His main conclusion, however, was that not only should the TCF contract be terminated and the money returned, but that the part of MCM's business plan oriented toward small business system markets should also be re-evaluated in view of the company's financial situation.

According to the estimates provided by Day, the prototype development of the MCM/170 would be as expensive as that of the MCM/70 and would take (under the most favourable conditions) approximately a quarter of the development time of the MCM/70. Furthermore, the MCM/170 simply could not be derived from the MCM/70, as the TCF business system requirements assumed data storage and processing capabilities that the MCM/70 could not provide, due mainly to the low speed of the 8008 processor.

While the $35,000 in seed money temporarily helped the company's cash flow problem, it became clear that continuing with the TCF contract would result in significant additional development costs which would not be recovered until the first TCF system was installed and working. In Day's opinion, the company simply could not afford that, as cash was low for even the completion of the production model of the MCM/70. MCM, he felt, should return the TCF advance and consider it not as a loss but as seven or eight months of free financing. Otherwise, the company was risking its entire future for the sake of $35,000. "Devoting less than all our development resources to the MCM/70 during the next 3–6 months," wrote Day, "considerably increases the risk of failing to get the /70 into volume production." Day continued his analysis with the call to reason.

There are only 3 things preventing us from doing whatever we want in new products; our ability to sell them, to make them and to finance ourselves. I see us presently committed to only one product – the basic MCM/70. Now is the time to fundamentally examine from the marketing, manufacturing, and financing perspectives, our business strategy ... To carry on with TCF at this time ... means risking our whole future for the sake of $35,000. Strategic decision-making for an ostensible multi-million dollar company should not be unduly influenced by $35,000.

Day's criticism went further, questioning the entire strategy of entering an established business systems market, a strategy which, in his opinion, was dangerous and unjustified in the case of MCM – a company that was yet to introduce its first product, and that for a different market niche. He reminded company managers that the marketing strategy that included the small business systems was formed in the early 1970s when "our expectations were that the MCM/70 processor could be used in these systems and that we would be currently selling 1,000 MCM/70s a month and wondering what to do with all the money pouring in, but the expectations were wrong and the strategy is obsolete."

In the end, Day's memo didn't have much effect on the termination of the TCF contract. To the best of the author's knowledge, the TCF system was never developed by MCM, but the MCM/170 concept reemerged a few years later as the MCM/800 computer.

There was no doubt within MCM's managerial ranks that a successful company ought to be always looking ahead to its next product and that the MCM/70 would have to be replaced, sooner rather than later, by a faster computer. Reports coming out from the National Computer Conference, which took place in Chicago in May 1974, clearly indicated that Intel's new and fast microprocessor – the 8080 – had already started to show up in computer hardware. R2E's Micral S, exhibited during the

Chicago show, was powered by the new microprocessor, replacing the older 8008 chip inside the Micral N, shown just a
few months earlier during the SICOB exhibit in Paris.

MCM's position on the 8080 issue is rather puzzling. The managers were aware of the superiority of the new chip from Intel
over the 8008 processor currently employed in the MCM/70.
And, for a short period of time, the company seemed to be committed to the development of the 8080-based successor to the
MCM/70. Some, like Laraya and Kutt, were strong proponents
of microprocessor technology. In notes taken during the 24
April managers' meeting, Kutt wrote that the company should
start work on the 8080 based machine as soon as possible.
However, for others, MCM's future was with more traditional
computer hardware technologies. Kutt strongly disagreed: "Yes,
this [8008 microprocessor] is slow but the next version, and the
next version are coming and we wouldn't have to do much [to
adapt them]."

During the 24 May managers' meeting, Ramer agreed to investigate and write a report on how the company might begin
manufacturing the next generation of its computers by 1975.
These computers were to be at least ten times faster than the
MCM/70 and capable of driving a multi-line display and using
floppy disk drives for virtual memory and storage. In his report *Micro Computer Machines: Development Policy*, Ramer
sketched two possible hardware development paths leading to
"a range of personal low-cost APL computers capable of driving a variety of peripherals, assuming and maintaining a leadership in this market niche created by the introduction of the
MCM/70."

From an overall point of view, both paths looked the same:
they both originated with the MCM/70, went through the
MCM/77 computer as an intermediate step, and ended with
the MCM/170 hardware. The MCM/77 was to be the ten times
faster refinement of the MCM/70. The greater data-handling ca-

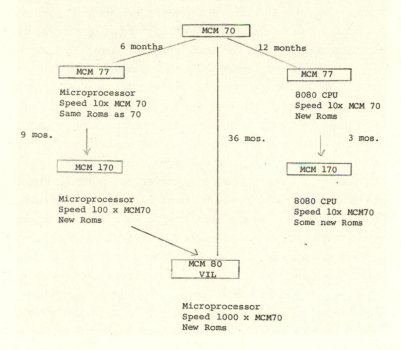

POSSIBLE DEVELOPMENT PATHS

Ramer's alternative paths for evolving new MCM computers from the MCM/70. (Source: Ramer, G., *Micro Computer Machines Inc. Development Policy*, 1974.)

pabilities of the /170 were to open new markets in commercial and scientific areas. The /170 would have at least 48K of RAM and would be able to drive multi-line displays, disk drives, and a variety of other peripherals. On the software side, the /170 was to offer state-of-the-art APL with MCM enhancements.

The two hardware development paths differed with respect to the underlying technology to be used to develop the MCM/77 and /170 computers. The first path assumed the use of the new Intel 8080 microprocessor as the CPU for both the MCM/77 and /170 computers. New APL software would have to be developed, but all application programs written for the MCM/70 would work on both of the new micros. The MCM/170 would not be significantly different from the /77 apart from some internal software to allow the use of more peripherals.

On the other hand, the second path assumed that the CPUs of the /77 and /170 computers would, informally speaking, be still like the 8008 but faster. (For more technically oriented readers: these CPUs were to be hardware emulations of the 8008 instruction set.) Such CPUs could be built even of discrete TTL (transistor-transistor logic) components. According to Ramer's calculations, the speed gains over the MCM/70 were a factor of ten for the /77 and of 100 for the /170 computer. While the /77 would work under the MCM/70 software, the /170 model would require a new version of the APL/AVS/EASY suite.

There is one more significant difference between the two paths. While the non-8080 approach continues toward yet another computer – the MCM/80, predicted to be 1,000 times faster than the MCM/70 – the 8080 path ends with the MCM/170. This indicated Ramer's uncertainty regarding the fate of microprocessor development at Intel. According to Ramer, it would be the MCM/80's role to "place MCM in a position where the Company can maintain the leadership in the field of personalized computers."

In Ramer's opinion, MCM's product development policies should have been based on the principle that the design of each new product would "take optimal advantage of the development effort of preceding products while heading as directly as possible to the Company's objectives." In this context, he explicitly endorsed the non-8080 approach to future hardware development, emphasizing that it was more "evolutionary"; the transformation of the MCM/70 into the /77 model could reuse as much hardware and software of the MCM/70 as possible, including the MCM APL/AVS/EASY software.

But Ramer's argument for abandoning the 8080 path was not without its flaws. The reason for building the MCM/70 around the microprocessor was not to satisfy Kutt's curiosity with respect to emerging semiconductor technologies; rather, it was to show that the microprocessor offered a revolutionary new approach to computer hardware design and that those who embarked on the microprocessor path had a great opportunity to renew the computer industry and to benefit from the potentially unlimited personal microcomputer market. The spirit of this product development philosophy is lost in Ramer's report, and so is the analysis of the microprocessor industry, which, when properly conducted, would show its rapid growth in terms of new microprocessors' capabilities and sales. By 1974, Intel was no longer the sole company in possession of the necessary technology for the volume manufacturing of four- and eight-bit microprocessors; Fairchild, Microsystems International, Motorola, National Semiconductor, Rockwell, Texas Instruments, and other semiconductor manufacturers were ready to supply the electronics industry with their microprocessor products. It was not a question of "if" but "when" the 8080 would be followed by even better chips.

Ramer was not against the 8080 approach. In fact, when the company decided to halt the development work on an 8080 machine during the 15 April managers' meeting, and it was agreed that the 8080 project "will be held in abeyance," Ramer pleaded for an early completion of the 8080 emulator to enable him to start on the 8080 APL software. This project, according to Ramer, would have to start in May in order to have software ready by the end of 1974. One may therefore interpret Ramer's rather conservative approach toward future hardware development at MCM, as represented by his report, as a plea to salvage as much of the hard work on the MCM/70 software done by his group as possible. Indeed, the use of the 8080 would require rewriting of the MCM APL/AVS/EASY software, and that required resources – perhaps the very resources that the company was wasting by investigating the possibility of patenting the bank switching technique it used in the MCM/70 to address the memory shortage problem. The new software destined for the 8080 CPU would dispose of bank switching altogether; the 8080 microprocessor could work directly with enough memory to comfortably host even Ramer's York APL.

Day's and Ramer's reports show how difficult it was for early microcomputer companies to anticipate the direction and rate of growth of the semiconductor industry and, hence, to have a well-developed business strategy that would translate the technological advancements offered by that industry into new opportunities in the educational, problem-solving, and business sectors of the computer market.

The early software and hardware development decisions made by MCM resulted in a remarkable product concept: the MCM/70. But later decisions to make it an even more compelling consumer electronics gadget not only delayed the computer's introduction into the market but also made it difficult to upgrade. Some of these choices seemed minor and inconsequential, such as the decision against installing an internal fan to remove the excessive heat from the MCM/70's case generated during the computer's operation and to seek alternative, "quiet" solutions instead. The main motivation for doing so was the desire to provide a user with a quiet operating environment. To solve the thermal problem without the use of a "noisy" fan, all the boards of the MCM/70 were packaged in iodized aluminum enclosures, clustered (or sandwiched) together and mounted on the back of the case. A large number of wires hung out of this pack of clustered casings in various directions, connecting the encased boards to the power supply, screen, cassette drives, keyboard, and other components of the computer. To replace a faulty PCB (printed circuit board), one had to remove the entire pack of casings from the computer, dismantle it into separate enclosures, peel the faulty board out of its aluminum enclosure, put in a new one, and repeat the described operations in reverse order. That was a very time-consuming process. Furthermore, the addition of new memory or interface boards was simply impossible without redesigning the entire thermal-protected pack of PCB casings.

The R2E Micral, on the other hand, was designed from the start with the objective of allowing flexible operation with a variety of peripherals that might require their own individual interface cards installed in the computer. What Gernelle, the main hardware engineer at R2E, came up with was a motherboard with a number of sockets mounted on it. One could plug all sorts of boards into these sockets, from CPU and memory boards to interface boards. (For those readers to whom computer architecture is not a mystery, the Micral had a 60-bit single data bus, called Pluribus, which could handle up to seven channels for fast peripherals, each channel having its own buffer memory.) To replace a Micral's faulty board or replace one with an upgrade, one had only to pull out the board to be replaced and push a new one into the desired socket. The operation took seconds. And yes, the Micral was equipped with an internal fan.

Ramer's *Development Policy* document was, of course, just a proposal, prepared under the rather heavy clouds that had started to descend upon MCM. It would not be worth an extended discussion if, in the end, MCM had not taken the very path he recommended – but with rather different results from those forecast in his report. The MCM/77 concept was released in 1976 as the MCM/800. It was ten times faster than the MCM/70, but its CPU was neither the 8080 nor any other microprocessor. The MCM/800 had to be packaged into a new case and it did have an internal fan. Because of its late release and lack of outstanding features, the computer was mostly unnoticed in the (by then) crowded market of small computers. Microprocessors had not disappeared, but instead had become even faster and even more popular. The Intel 8080A, Motorola

6800, and Zilog z80 microprocessors had become the micro-computer industry's de facto standards and were working inside general-purpose computers all over the world.

Sharing the power —
the venture capital way

To raise its operating capital, MCM tapped into various sources of financing, from bank lines of credit and contracts from other companies, to sales of the company's common shares and venture capital investments. Of all these financing options, venture capital sponsorship had the largest impact on the company's corporate history.

In 1972, Kutt attracted the attention of a group of individuals associated with the Toronto law firm Borden, Elliot, Kelley & Palmer, later renamed as Borden & Elliot Barristers and Solicitors. He impressed them with his personal computer ideas, which he illustrated with the cardboard mockup of the MCM/70, and they agreed to provide venture capital through purchasing KSI's common shares. The "outside shareholders," as the group, extended by other names, would refer to itself in some future documents, consisted initially of Vermay Investments Ltd, B.V. Elliot, W.S. Robertson, and J.T. Johnson. For Kutt and KSI, the participation of outside investors in KSI's financial program was a promise of steady financing, bank loan guarantees, and, through the association with Borden & Elliot, legal services.

In December 1972, the founding group of outside shareholders purchased 6,290 common shares of KSI at $9 per share with the right to purchase an additional 6,290 at the same price until the end of September 1974. According to the letter from Robertson to Kutt, dated 21 December 1972, this was to be "the first step in what, it is hoped by all, will be an extensive participation in the company's financial program."

Venture capital investments had usually been high risk and therefore it was not unusual to expect that the outside shareholders group would want some control over KSI's decision-making process to protect its investment. To that end, there was some hard work ahead of the group, since all corporate powers resided with Kutt. He was the president and the only director of the company. That gave him sole power over the company's business operations, including the defining and assigning responsibilities to the officers of the company. He also owned a large majority of KSI's common shares, which gave him full control over the company's constitution and general policies, such as the election of the company's officers and the setting up of authorized capital for the corporation by creating common shares. It was only inevitable that the outside shareholders group would apply pressure on Kutt on a number of fronts to erode his powers as well as his share-holding domination.

Increasing the number of KSI directors was not a difficult issue. Kutt understood quite well that, in the long run, a corporation such as MCM could not function properly with a one-person board of directors. However, Kutt agreed not only to an increase in the number of directors but also to the outside shareholders' request that they should have the right to nominate one director of the company. During the 8 December 1972 shareholders' meeting, several by-laws were passed, the most important of which increased the number of directors from one to five, and increased the authorized capital of the corporation by creating an additional 1,750,000 common shares without per value to total 2,000,000.

In February 1973, KSI, renamed as Micro Computer Machines Inc., appointed two new directors, W.S. Robertson and M.L. Davies, and in May the board welcomed its fourth member, W.H. Thompson.

To pay its bills, MCM needed more money and was looking for ways of raising $300,000 of additional capital at a minimum

Micro Computer Machines common share. (Source: York University Computer Museum.)

cost to the company. MCM could sell 30,000 common shares at, say, $10 a share. Or, it could prevent share dilution by arranging a bank line of credit for the required amount, guaranteed by some of the existing shareholders. In return, the guarantors would immediately receive some nominal number of shares and, later, some additional shares for each day the guarantees were in effect, according to some agreed-upon formula. The latter solution not only seemed more beneficial to the shareholders but could also be implemented with some of the outside shareholders as guarantors.

In March, Kutt met with Robertson at dinner to discuss a possible way to arrange a guaranteed line of credit. That meeting was followed by further discussions with Robertson and B.V. Elliot, and these in turn resulted in the agreement signed on 7 April which paved the way to a $235,000 line of credit from the Toronto Dominion Bank, guaranteed by the same initial group of outside shareholders which, in MCM documents, is referred to as the "guarantors." But to close the deal, Kutt agreed to a number of concessions requested by the guarantors. He agreed to vote his shares so that "a majority of the board of directors shall be persons nominated by or acceptable to the present shareholders of the Company who are not employees or officers of the Company." If there were any doubts about the intended meaning of that assurance, they were dispersed by the wording of the amendment to the 7 April agreement proposed to Kutt in October. This time around, Kutt was to agree to vote his shares so that "a majority of directors shall be nominated by or acceptable to the majority of common shares held by the 'outside shareholders' of the Company." The document also specifies who these "outside shareholders" were, and the number of MCM's common shares owned by each of the eighteen members of the group. From that data, it had to be obvious to Kutt that the MCM common shares owned by guarantors, namely by Vermay Investments, Robertson, and Elliot, would, if voted together, constitute such a majority of shares.

In all fairness, the proposed amendment offered ways to withhold the assurance in question: go public with MCM, or offer to buy the outside shareholders out for $20 per share and $11 per right to purchase a share – both highly unlikely at that stage of the company's development. To buy the shareholders out, Kutt would have to deposit $528,410 in cash, almost twice the amount of the line of credit backed by the guarantors. In short, if Kutt agreed to the amendment, the board of directors would be in the hands of the outside shareholders. He did agree, not knowing that his signature endorsing the amended agreement would cost him his presidency a few months later and the company its leadership position in the emerging microcomputer market.

The $235,000 in line-of-credit funds could keep MCM going only for a few months, since, in early 1974, the company was spending an average of $60,000 a month. To start the volume production of the MCM/70, which was now projected to begin in mid-1974, the company needed more cash. A new agreement between Kutt and the same group of guarantors, reached in March 1974, called for an increase of the bank line of credit by an additional $180,000. These extended loan guarantees, however, would not come cost-free to Kutt, as he was asked to make further concessions. This time, he was to forgo his monthly salary of $3,000, effective 1 April 1974, until the production of the MCM/70 began. The foregone salary was to be regarded as a loan to MCM and was to be repaid by the company as soon as MCM was in a financial position to do so and only after the guaranteed bank loan was repaid. "In consideration of making such loans," wrote Robertson in his 14 March 1974 letter to Kutt, "you shall be entitled to receive, commencing with the initial utilization of the credit ... shares of the company on the same basis as granted to the guarantors of such increased line of credit."

Robertson's letter to Kutt explicitly stated that the additional loan could only be used to pay for purchase of inventory needed to start the production of the MCM/70. Furthermore, before MCM could draw funds from this additional loan, W. Thompson (an MCM director) would have to provide the board of directors with the results of the testing of an MCM/70 carried out by his company.

The spirit of the new agreement indicated the outside shareholders' concern with the Company's ability to move quickly into production. The general market conditions were bad. Since 1973, the stock market had been going through what was historically one of its most severe and prolonged declines; before everything was over, technology stocks would plummet more than 60 per cent. In that climate, so unfavourable for investors, the guarantors wanted Kutt to share more financial responsibilities for product development. After all it was he who, as the majority shareholder, had the most to gain by bringing the MCM/70 swiftly to production readiness.

Kutt objected to strict restrictions on the use of additional funds, knowing that the largest single expense was employee salaries. However, his attempt at controlling this expenditure by eliminating non-essential jobs was, according to Kutt, rejected by the board of directors.

Robertson's 14 March letter to Kutt also confirmed that Kutt was in accord with the suggestion that Bruce C. Wallace be appointed to fill the vacancy on the board of directors. Wallace was not a stranger to Kutt nor to anybody else at MCM. In 1972, he was taken out of semi-retirement and parachuted into MCM territory by the outside shareholders. According to Kutt, he wasn't an MCM employee, he was just a person associated with the company's most important financial backers. "He was never on staff," said Kutt. "We never paid him anything. I just let him come in." His initially peculiar presence at MCM became, in time, a part of its corporate culture. There is no explicit evidence to support the hypothesis that Wallace's initial assignment was to gather intelligence on MCM's activities. However, Wallace's constant presence at MCM soon began to produce results in the form of alliances with some of the MCM employees. According to Kutt, these alliances played a significant role in his own power struggle with the outside shareholders and, in some important cases, would misguide the board of directors in their decision-making process. "They believed him more than they ever should," concluded Kutt.

Wallace became an MCM director on 2 April 1974. Soon after Wallace's appointment, it became completely evident to Kutt that his own control over the board of directors had been lost to the outside shareholders. The financial situation of the company wasn't improving, and the company was burning money faster than Kutt was able to supply it. The beginning of volume production of the MCM/70 was rescheduled, yet again, to August. Kutt had no choice but to propose stiff reductions to the board. He also reported to the directors that work on an advanced power supply for the MCM computer was holding up the final phase of the computer's development and should be terminated. According to Kutt, the board rejected both requests. The company's operating budgets for June and July were $51,000 and $57,600, respectively, while the completion of the power supply was continually delayed.

What happened next came as a gift from the employees to the outside shareholders group. It came in the form of a managerial revolt against Kutt, against his way of managing the company and dealing with its employees. The managers' main concern was the lack of transparent organizational structure and of solid day-to-day management of the company. They also wanted pay raises and more company shares allocated to them. All of a sudden, everybody was discussing major managerial reforms: directors at board meetings, managers during their management committee meetings, some directors with some managers at pre-arranged meetings, and, it seems, almost everybody else with anybody else who still didn't have enough of corporate politicking.

During the 24 May management committee meeting, the participants agreed to support the directors' position that "the company must institute a sound fundamental project-control orientation to provide sufficiently accurate data for making financial forecasts." The managers agreed to set to work immediately on the implementation of this policy based on the *Philosophy of Project Control* document prepared and distributed by Thompson, one of the company's directors. In his document, Thompson laid down the principles for having all the company's activities under verifiable control to allow for planning and forecasting.

During the 24 May meeting, the managers anonymously passed a cost-of-living salary adjustment resolution, demanding an increase of 0.8 per cent per month since each employee's last salary adjustment. Did they have a complete financial picture of the corporation? Did they know that the extended line of credit, still awaiting the Bank's final approval, could not be used to pay for salaries, and that Kutt had stopped receiving his own? Kutt was absent from the meeting, but Wallace, a director of the company with full knowledge of MCM's financial standing, was not.

Everybody wanted a chief operating officer to run MCM's day-to-day operations: the directors wanted it, the managers wanted it, and even Kutt was not opposed to the idea of bringing in a CEO to assume, under the president's supervision and subject to the ultimate control of the board, full responsibility for the operations of the company. Reg Rea was doing that successfully at the Kingston plant and he could, at least temporarily, have filled the much-needed CEO position. Unfortunately, his managerial skills went unnoticed.

Dissatisfaction with Kutt in the managerial ranks started to resemble open revolt. In June, nine of the core members of MCM wrote a memo to the board of directors requesting that Bruce Wallace, rather than Kutt, represent their interests as shareholders on the board of directors. During the June board of directors meeting, Kutt was informed that certain management personnel were dissatisfied with the way Kutt was running MCM. He was told about meetings between those employees and certain directors where dissatisfaction was openly expressed. In Kutt's view, the source of the negative feelings was primarily discontent with salaries; certain employees "wanted to buy more common shares of the Company that I had previously agreed to sell to them."

In July 1974, the crisis reached its climax. In the 3 July letter sent by the Managers Committee to the board of directors, the managers wrote,

The company during the past several months has gone
through considerable upset and turmoil in the managerial
ranks. In May and early June, representation was made
personally to some of the board members about these
problems without the knowledge of all the board members. As we understand it, the board in its June meeting
insisted that any internal problems first be dealt with internally and only if they cannot satisfactorily be resolved
in that way, that they then should be brought to the board.
Attempts at accommodating the situation internally have
been made, but the upset has not gone away and both the
individuals involved and the company are suffering for it.
We request that as a final effort to reach a resolution to
our problems, that the board personally interview each of
the managers, assess our individual and collective griev-
ances and our individual competences (as much as you are
able). After hearing us out, it is our hope that the decision
of the board will then be accepted as the conclusion of
these matters and all the individuals involved will return
to devoting their whole energies to the interests of the
company.

The managers' wish was granted and on 15 July, Kutt sent a
memo informing them about their individual meetings with
the board, which would take place on 16 July, starting at 10:30
A.M., one half hour per individual. The managers listed in
Kutt's memo were: Mike Day, Ted Edwards, José Laraya, Gord
Ramer, Reg Rea, Morgan Smyth, and Peter Wolfe. Kutt's desperate attempt to address the managers before the meeting was
futile. No board member, including Kutt, was allowed to talk
with employees before the 16 July meeting. That did not prevent
employees from organizing further meetings. In his corporate
notes, Kutt entered: "Mike [Day] said BD [Board of Directors]

instructed him to set up meetings & make [them] look like employees asked [for them]."

Emotions were growing exponentially with every hour approaching the 16 July meeting. Kutt tried to talk to some of the managers but couldn't get far. He wrote in his notes that Ramer definitely felt everything would be resolved on 16 July and, hopefully, with only a few casualties. In anticipation of the outcome, Kutt added: "Whatever [the] outcome, some people will resign & that is unfortunately the case."

If MCM's board of directors had held constitutional power to strip Kutt from his presidency, that would most likely have been the outcome of the 16 July meeting with managers. Instead, the board did the second best thing, by stripping the office of the president of all effective powers in running the company. The board passed a new by-law amending By-law No. 1 of the Company. According to the amendment, "the President of the Company shall only have such duties and responsibilities as are from time to time assigned to him by the board of directors of the Company." During the meeting, the board appointed Wallace as the Managing Director of MCM, with full authority and responsibility for the operation of the company. The powers and responsibilities of the newly created position were made subject to the authority of the board of directors only, and not to the supervision of the president.

Detailed instructions were dispatched to handle Kutt's dismissal. An unsigned MCM document, addressed possibly to MCM clerical stuff, detailed permissible responses to inquiries about Kutt. For phone calls:

1   Inquire as to the caller's name and company name.
2   If the caller indicates it is a personal call, then refer him
    to Mers Kutt's home phone number 449-5658.

3 If it is a business call or you have any doubts that it is
   a personal call then respond with: "Mr. Bruce Wallace
   has been recently appointed as Managing Director of the
   company and will be handling all of Mr. Kutt's calls."
4 If the caller inquires as to M.K.'s status, respond with:
   "Mr. Kutt remains as President of the company, but all
   operating authority now resides with Mr. Wallace."
5 Any further probing on the part of the caller should be
   responded to with: "I cannot answer your questions. If
   you would direct your questions to Mr. Wallace, he may
   be able to answer them."
6 Transfer call to Bruce or take a message.

For "General Conversation with Outsiders" the document in-
sists on responding only with "Mr. Bruce Wallace has been
recently appointed as Managing Director of the company. Mr.
Kutt remains as President, but all operating authority now resides with Mr. Wallace." No further information was to be vol-
unteered.

Kutt made no entry in his corporate notebook on 16 July, or
on any of the following five days. On Sunday, 21 July, he wrote:
"Gord Ramer ... [he] knew it was in [the] wind. Wanted it to
happen but not at that time." Kutt ended the entry with a desperate plea: "Everyone [is] getting sick of [MCM/]70 ... morale
down. Help."

The extent of the damage that the 16 July decision to strip Kutt
of his presidential powers would inflict on MCM was so easy to
predict that one may wonder by what sound method of reasoning the board of directors arrived at its drastic decision. First,
Kutt's humiliation could not possibly end the power struggle
between him and the outside shareholders, but only lift it to
another level. After all, he insisted that the 16 July decision to

remove the powers and duties of the president – preventing him from supervising MCM's operations – and the appointment of Wallace as managing director constituted, from a legal point of view, wrongful dismissal from his presidential office. Furthermore, his pockets were still full of controlling shares and he could use shareholders' meetings as a new battlefield. In a fast-moving high technology sector such as computing, extended delays in product development could be devastating. The little window of opportunity that was left to MCM in mid-1974 was shrinking fast, and the company simply could not afford an idle mode of operations, chewing on what was left of the bank line of credit in anticipation of some political resolve. Finally, the replacement of Kutt with the inexperienced Wallace could not clear the employees' discontent with their financial or corporate standing, nor remove the production bottlenecks; it could only endanger the deals with the distributors, the company's only hope for survival.

It is of limited historical value to pose questions such as whether Kutt could have prevented the 16 July disaster, whether he could have effectively addressed the employees' discontent, or have found ways to work more effectively with the venture capital group. In the end, in the most crucial moment, he found himself isolated both on the board of directors and within the managerial group of MCM. He wasn't getting adequate legal and corporate advice to help him properly assess and act upon the actions taken by the outside shareholders' group. If he were to survive and fight back, he would have to rebuild the neglected alliances – and fast.

The power supply that blacked out MCM

At the beginning of 1974, there were still a number of hardware-related problems that MCM had to address before starting the volume manufacturing of its computer. The company was still searching for a supplier of ROMs with the MCM/70's software programmed into them. The new computer case needed some final design touches, and the electric motor that was to operate the cassette drive of the computer proved to be inadequate. Finally, the machine was awaiting a new power supply. Under normal conditions, all these problems could have been resolved within eight to ten weeks. And most of them were. Unfortunately, the computer's power supply, whose design, testing, redesign, and retesting dragged on for months, became one of the factors that brought the MCM/70 project to the verge of collapse in the second half of 1974.

The answer to the question of what went wrong with the power supply project seems to be more complex than the power supply itself, and to tackle it, one has to go back to mid-1973 and the second wave of MCM's recruitment efforts. In retrospect, one of Kutt's biggest mistakes on the hiring front was the job offer made to Edward (Ted) Murray Edwards in July 1973, soon after the APL Conference in Toronto. It was not because Edwards lacked professional competence. On the contrary, he was a gifted and knowledgeable individual who had a Master's degree in Science from the University of British Columbia and a fair share of experience in the academic as well as the business world. He was a first-rate APLer, too. In 1971 he joined Control Data Canada (CDC) in Mississauga, Ontario, and by the following year he was responsible for all APL implementation activities for Control Data Corporation, CDC's parent company. He and his team at CDC were developing APL*STAR software for Control Data Corporation's Star series computers. But the Star hardware project was on rather shaky ground and, in spite of good progress on APL*STAR's implementation, Edwards' group was to be reassigned to another project that he was less than enthusiastic about. In May of 1973, at the APL conference in Toronto, he learned about the APL efforts at MCM and decided to leave CDC.

But what exactly was he to do at MCM, which, in 1973, was simply too small to embrace all the engineering talent that Edwards and his group represented? In spite of his considerable APL expertise, Edwards could not be explicitly involved in the development of the MCM/APL code; Ramer would simply not have it. Before joining CDC, Edwards taught electronic circuit design in the Electrical Engineering Department at the University of Alberta. But all the top hardware positions at MCM were already occupied. Laraya was running the show and was quite unhappy when Kutt brought Reg Rea to MCM and put him in charge of Kingston operations as vice-president of engineering. In the end, the two men managed to work things out and collaborated smoothly. There was obviously no place for a third hardware engineer in a leading role.

It is unclear what compelled Kutt to hire Edwards and two others from his APL group at CDC, Glen Seeds and Jim Litchfield. Was it their expertise and enthusiasm for APL work? Or was it perhaps the thrill of luring an entire APL development team away from one of the largest computer manufacturers? In the end, Edwards became a vice-president responsible for planning. In 1973, he played a significant role in bringing the MCM/70 to the attention of research and academic communities. Of course, giving MCM/70 seminars would never be a substitute for creative software or hardware engineering work and, hence, when the power supply project was up for grabs, Edwards agreed to lead its development.

All electronic equipment requires electrical energy to power its internal components, and a power supply is a device that provides that energy. A power supply can do more than just provide electrical current of a specified type and parameters; it can manage and control the overall power consumption, and it can even protect an electronic device from damage due to overheating or sudden power fluctuations or interruptions.

The MCM/70 power supply project might seem only a peripheral assignment compared to the major hardware and software tasks at MCM, such as the development of the memory management system or the design and implementation of MCM/APL. But it was not. The MCM/70 was to be a small and portable computer, and that constrained the size and weight of its power supply. Traditional power supply designs of that time called for heavy and large modules with one or more fans to remove the excess heat generated by the electronic and other electrical components of a computer. These power supplies were not very efficient either. Only sixty to seventy per cent of the energy that entered such a power supply left it in a useful form; the rest, converted to heat, was lost.

With a traditional design, to keep MCM's computer small, the power supply would have to be, for instance, taken outside of the computer and hosted in a separate enclosure. The computer would have to be connected with a special cable to the power supply box in order to provide the various voltages required by the computer's hardware. On the other hand, a built-in power supply for a typewriter-sized MCM/70 would require the use of new technologies to increase its power efficiency to as much as 90 per cent. "The power supply was a big challenge," commented Laraya. Edwards' proposal for a small, highly efficient power supply inside the computer was elegant and gained the company's endorsement. "It was interesting," continued Laraya. "We were pushing the technology there using CMOS [Complementary Metal-Oxide Semiconductor technology]. CMOS was in its early stages as well. Because being a portable machine, we wanted a very low power dissipation."

Edwards was initially instructed to build a simple but efficient power supply. But very quickly new features were added to the design, making the power supply project a more and more ambitious undertaking. First, it was decided not to install any fans inside the MCM/70 to vent the heat from the computer. It was predicted that with the high target efficiency for the proposed power supply, the computer would not overheat and, without a fan, would be as quiet as a pocket calculator. The only noise coming out of the machine would be the soothing sound of a spinning tape inside the machine's tape drive.

Another added design feature was a power failure protection capability. It would allow continuous operation of the MCM/70 under battery power in the event of power failure. For an extended power loss, the computer would initiate an orderly shutdown: it would automatically provided system back-up by copying the content of computer's RAM to cassette before it terminated all its operations. The system would be automatically reinstated when the power was restored and batteries were recharged.

The proposed switching power supply for the MCM/70 was a very ambitious proposal that got many people excited. But not all. Rea was of an opinion that "in the first version [of MCM/70] we shouldn't worry about things like no fan. And between Ted [Edwards] and the boys they wanted a machine that was totally silent, no fan." Kutt and Laraya also preferred a more cautious approach and would rather have seen the first batch of MCM/70s powered by an efficient internal power supply without added features that only required additional time and resources to develop and, according to Rea, "shouldn't have been a hold-up for the first version of the machine." Laraya concurred:

We could work on that later … In fact, I was a big proponent of that [cautious approach to the power supply development]. We were pushing the technology on switching power supplies with everything else and yet there was an argument to be made for a hybrid type of supply, perhaps

not as efficient, not the 80–90 per cent efficiency that
the switching power supply [aimed at], maybe something
like 60 per cent, so there is a bit more heat, perhaps you
needed a fan.

The variants of the advanced power supply either did not
work properly or worked briefly as prototypes but could not
be converted into a stable product. By mid-1974, Kutt's frustration with the power supply situation reached the point that he
urged the board of directors to take Edwards off the project.
In his corporate notes, he wrote that he could easily sell the
computer with its original simple power supply. At this stage,
he noted, "who needs the advanced power supply?" But despite
Kutt's technical and entrepreneurial knowledge, the board decided against his advice and allowed the advanced power supply
project to continue. This was a surprising decision in view of
MCM's worsening financial situation. According to Kutt, it was
Wallace who, influenced by Edwards, was continuously providing an optimistic assessment of the power supply project to the
directors. Kutt, already isolated on the board, could only watch
in frustration.

The subsequent reports from Edwards pushed the completion of the supply from May to June, then from June to July.
Concerned with the delays, Rea and Laraya decided to look for
an alternative, "brute force" power supply to be used with the
MCM/70 in the event of further delays to the main power supply
project. They visited a power supply design house in Toronto
and provided it with specifications for an alternative power
supply for the MCM/70. "And I got a quote and, I think, even a
prototype," recalled Rea. "I presented it to the executive committee [of managers] as a backup and I was thrown out ... This
was sacrilege to suggest this kind of switching power supply.
So it died right there. But I think José and I kept it in the background, kept dealing with these [power supply] people, making

sure that everything was alive, to be able to turn [things] on at the right time."

The 16 July dethroning of Kutt did not resolve the power supply issue: the MCM/70 was ready but still awaiting a reliable power supply. The company was divided, unable to heal, and without any effective management from Wallace who, as the Managing Director, was still unable to correctly assess the situation and make any decisive moves. On the other hand, a growing number of MCM employees, concerned that the power supply situation was critically endangering the company's very existence, were taking independent action. "What we need ... is a 'stupid' brute force power supply [as opposed to Edwards' 'smart' switching power supply]," wrote Laraya in his memo to Wallace. "We should use this type until we are able to get something better." On 1 August, a group of twenty-two MCM employees sent a memo to the board of directors. In the memo, which begins

> To the members of the Board of Directors of Micro Computer Machines, Inc.
>
> In the earnest belief that it is for the betterment of Micro Computer Machines Inc., we the undersigned, unsolicited, submit the following resolutions.

the employees demanded an end to the power supply dispute, beginning with cutting Edwards off from any direct involvement with the mainstream, ongoing product development and production decisions. The plans for yet another redesign of the power supply, proposed by Edwards, were to be immediately terminated and a simple solution to the power supply problem found.

There was no immediate response from the board to the 1 August memo. To assemble new machines, the managers had no

A promotional photograph of an early MCM/70 demonstrator.
(Source: York University Computer Museum, photographer
unknown.)

choice but to order Power Conversion Systems Ltd to assemble
60 power supplies of Edwards' design. According to Laraya,
that decision was made "on the basis of Mr. Edwards claiming
that the power supplies would work if not for assembly errors."
But only two days after that decision was made, on 16 August,
Edwards issued a report about the status of the power supply.
His document indicated a variety of "clean-up problems" and
asserted that the power supply problem would be solved by
12 September in time for MCM's trip to its largest distributor
client, ILC Data Device Corporation (DDC) of Hickville, New
York. Since May, DDC had been lining up potential buyers of
the MCM/70 and was optimistic about the computer's sales in
the United States.

On 17 September, an MCM team traveled to DDC to demonstrate a number of MCM/70s during a week-long seminar/trade

show. The very survival of MCM hinged upon DDC's volume sales of MCM/70s. In general, the DDC salesmen were enthusiastic about the machines; some of them took the MCM/70s to their hotel rooms to play with overnight. However, the number of power-supply-related failures during the show was alarming. Furthermore, DDC informed MCM that barely three days after the show "unit no. 4 (which, incidentally, was claimed to have the 'best' power supply), was down because of a blown power supply. Smoke came out of one of the coils ... Unit no. 7 was down because it kept on blowing fuses."

On 24 September, several employees, including Laraya and Rea, wrote a report on the status of the power supply and its impact on the company's survival. In the document, the authors reported that Edwards' "clean-up" of the power supply not only missed the 12 September deadline, but also that "The 'clean-up' referred to in the 16 August memo turned out to be a redesign of the controller." The authors complained that "there is no complete documentation on why changes were made and what problems these changes were supposed to solve." (It is surprising that MCM was unable to institute and enforce such requirements for all its research and development activities.)

But that was not the end of the critical report. The authors pointed out that the "switching inverter techniques used by Mr. Edwards had already been published by Motorola in many of their Application Notes in 1972 and also by Electronics magazine in 1973." According to the authors, "these were not taken advantage of."

The report also quoted the opinion of Power Conversion Systems Ltd (PCSL) which was critical of MCM's switching power supply. Apparently, even if PCSL agreed to manufacture these advanced power supplies designed at MCM, PCSL would be unable to provide a guarantee for them. PCSL informed the authors of the report that they had experience with these types of power supplies and that it would take the company approxi-

September 24, 1974

RECOMMENDATIONS:

1)   The "Brute Force" power supply should be committed to an outside group
      without any involvement of Mr. Edwards.

      Mr. Laraya, Vice President, Engineering, should have sole responsibility
      for the project and units would be reliably available in October.

2)   Current internal redesign of the power supply should be terminated.

3)   Current management structure is not solving the problems.
      Mers Kutt if reinstated can give the required leadership.

24 September power supply recommendations signed by eighteen MCM
employees. (Source: M. Kutt's archive.)

mately 8 to 10 weeks to completely design them and to set up its manufacturing. This was a fraction of the time spent by Edwards and his group. The authors concluded their report with the resolution: "We, therefore, contend that current redesign of the power supply be terminated, and that the final power supply should be designed, built, tested and guaranteed by Power Conversion Systems Ltd. We have better things to do."

Finally, it was evident even to Wallace that the power supply problem had shut the company down and created a serious financial crisis. The next day, on 25 September, he wrote to the directors urging them to attend the 1 October meeting and look for a firm financial rescue plan. "I believe you are aware that ... the production machines from our August schedule almost all had broken down due, among other things, to a failure of the power supply." It was possibly more due to the imminent financial collapse of the company than pressure from employees that the decision to postpone in-house development of the switching power supply in favor of a simpler "brute" version was finally made by the board of directors on 1 October. The directors also agreed that the decision for approving the new power supply would lie with Laraya.

But before MCM/70s equipped with a new power supply started to leave the manufacturing plant in Kingston, a number of key employees would empty their desks at MCM and leave the company. Mike Day, Mers Kutt, Reg Rea, and Morgan Smyth would not see the MCM/70s with "Made in Canada" stickers leaving the Kingston plant and entering the new personal computer market that those people had helped to define.

6

Changing Fortunes

In the end, the 16 July corporate shuffle at MCM had resolved
none of the controversial issues and failed to steer the company
out of its self-destructive mode of operations. Kutt remained the
company's president and a majority shareholder, but his managerial powers had been pared to the bone. The outside investors
were in full control of MCM's operations, from the board of
directors' functions down to day-to-day managerial decision-
making. But their long term ambitions remained constrained by
their minority shareholding position.

The new managerial regime under Wallace met on 21 July;
present were Day, Edwards, Victor Waese, Wallace, and Wolfe.
The main issue they discussed was an offer by Ted Berg of DDC
to visit MCM and help the company with its managerial problems in order to bring the MCM/70's development up to the production stage. Berg was deeply concerned with MCM's inability
to attack and resolve its internal problems. However, he was
still optimistic about the MCM/70's prospects in the marketplace and wanted seventy-five of these machines for DDC by
the end of 1974. Berg's visit was scheduled for 24 July. During
the meeting, it was decided that, in preparation for Berg's visit,
production issues should be given top priority. Furthermore,
to stress how serious and precarious the corporate situation

was, Wallace suggested keeping detailed logs of all decisions in the event that legal action were to be brought by shareholders against MCM.

The employees were mostly unaware of the nature and extent of the power struggle between Kutt and the outside investors. Some of them were being used as pawns in the game for corporate dominance, while others became increasingly proactive in search of realistic solutions to the most critical production bottlenecks. Their dissatisfaction with the corporate governance had not subsided, but the employees now seemed more organized and determined to act. They didn't want individual meetings with the directors anymore. Being more and more distrustful of the board's ability to correctly assess MCM's corporate and production realities, the employees began issuing resolutions. In their 1 August memo addressed to the board, twenty-two employees requested that MCM's "administration adopt a mechanism for making responsible and positive decisions based upon direct consultation with the personnel knowledgeable in the areas concerned." The employees also asked for full support for Rea and Laraya in their positions as vice-presidents responsible for manufacturing and development engineering, respectively. Their demands included strong managerial decisions to freeze the design of the current MCM/70 product, and a decisive commitment to budget and production schedules based on an accurate understanding of the company's production capabilities and market needs. Most importantly, they urged the board to resolve the critical issue of the MCM/70's power supply. They wanted a fast and simple solution and called for disengaging Edwards from any direct involvement with ongoing product development and production decisions.

But the solutions Wallace had in mind to address the company's managerial problems were entirely different. In his memo of 4 August, he announced to the employees a new organiza-

tional structure which couldn't possibly satisfy them: he gave
Edwards, not Laraya, Ramer, or Rea, the main responsibility
for MCM's new hardware and software directions. Wallace
appointed Edwards as vice-president of research and development, giving him sole responsibility for new product design and
initial development to the prototype stage. Edwards was now
in charge of the MCM/APL language and, in addition, was expected to investigate new technologies. Ramer was appointed
the manager of MCM's Kingston branch and the adviser to the
president on all technical matters of concern to the company,
possibly to compensate for his loss of control of APL's development. Laraya, however, kept his vice-president's title but saw his
assigned responsibilities greatly diminished, reduced mostly to
managing the engineering of products turned over by Edwards'
research and development group.

Wallace's reorganization did not help to bring MCM any
closer to manufacturing its computer in volume, raising even
more concerns about the future of the company among its employees. In another document issued by eighteen employees on
24 September, the signatories recommended once more that the
development of the brute force power supply be assigned to an
outside developer and that Laraya be given sole responsibility
for the power supply project. They also wanted Kutt to come
back, claiming that the "current management structure is not
solving the problems. Mers Kutt if reinstated can give the required leadership."

However, these recommendations, resolutions, and demands
were never given serious consideration. In his 30 September
memo to employees, Laraya reported on his meeting with Wallace which had taken place four days earlier. "During this conversation," he wrote, "I was directed to tell all the employees
who signed the 'petition' that after 1 October 1974, either himself or Mr. Mers Kutt would be sitting in the Managing Direc-

tor's chair. In either case Mr. Bruce Wallace said he did not 'give a damn.'"

I do have a fighting position

Meanwhile Kutt, who was largely disengaged from the employees' actions, was scrupulously planning his next moves. "I had my priorities," explained Kutt, "survival was number one." He understood well that the only cards he could play against the guarantors with some confidence were his majority shares. Hence, all his future actions had to be carefully crafted so as not to jeopardize his controlling position. Kutt also decided to channel all his negotiations with the board and the guarantors through Peter G. Beattie, a lawyer with the Toronto law firm McCarthy & McCarthy.

By mid-August, Kutt came up with three alternative strategies to resolve his conflict with the outside investors. The first one aimed at reducing, or eliminating altogether, the company's financial dependency on the guarantors. Another plan was to negotiate the so-called Kutt/MCM Agreement, the gist of which was the trading of Kutt's controlling shares for his exclusive rights to sell MCM products outside of North America. Kutt's final plan was to attack the guarantors directly by strengthening the company's by-laws to assure a strong presidential office controlled not by the board of directors but by shareholders. Since Kutt controlled the majority of the company's common shares, he could, after the successful passing of the by-laws in question, simply vote himself back into power. Kutt would, in fact, vigorously pursue all of these plans, eventually bringing the conflict with the guarantors to a head on 25 October in the Toronto office of Borden & Elliot.

But the climactic events of 25 October were still more than two months away. On 19 August, Kutt instructed Beattie, his counsel, to probe the guarantors' interest in either selling their shares to him or, at least, getting off the line of credit guarantees. He suggested that he could possibly offer them $500,000, one half immediately upon closing the deal, and the rest later according to a mutually agreed upon schedule. Unfortunately, after several meetings with the guarantors Beattie had nothing optimistic to report: the guarantors seemed uninterested in getting out of MCM or giving up control of the company. That deeply upset Kutt, as the rejection of his offer shattered any hopes for a fast and non-confrontational solution to the conflict.

"I'm biggest loser," wrote Kutt in his notes, reminiscing about his August meetings with Beattie. He concluded that selling his stock in the company was the best move for him. What he had in mind was selling 100,000 of his shares for $4 per share. That would mean, of course, losing his majority shareholding position. He would keep $56,000 to himself and would offer the remaining $344,000 to purchase the rights from MCM to manufacture and sell MCM products through a new company he would form and call MCM International. That was the Kutt/MCM Agreement in a nutshell. "I'm discussing with the other directors and some major shareholders the concept of the 'MCM/Kutt Agreement,'" wrote Robertson to Beattie on 22 August, acknowledging the receipt of Kutt's proposal.

A few days later, Kutt learned about the rejection of his Kutt/MCM Agreement in Robertson's 26 August letter to Beattie. "I have now had an opportunity to speak to the other directors and some major shareholders of MCM regarding the 'MCM/Kutt Agreement,'" wrote Robertson. "Their reaction to the draft ... [of the Agreement] was uniformly negative." It is likely that the proposed agreement was seen by the guarantors as Kutt's attempt to irritate them rather than to solve the conflict constructively. According to the proposed Kutt/MCM Agreement, Kutt was to give up his controlling shares for the right to establish MCM International, fully independent of MCM, but with rights to manufacture, modify, market, and sub-license all existing and future MCM products for all countries except Canada and the United States. Kutt wanted guaranteed access to all technical and cost data relevant to MCM's products, their development, and their manufacturing. According to the proposed agreement, he would be permitted to send observers to MCM who would then have free access to all documentation and data, and would be granted technical consultation, if requested. And that was not all. Kutt would remain an MCM director.

The Kutt/MCM Agreement was further discussed during the 5 September meeting of the board. The directors reviewed at length a memorandum submitted by Kutt's counsel dealing with the proposal that "the Company enter into an agreement with Mr. Kutt granting him an exclusive distributorship for all MCM products for the world exclusive of North America for a consideration to be satisfied by the surrender by him to the Company of certain shares of the Company owned by him." It was agreed that further discussions would take place with the objective of achieving agreement not later than 16 September. But that deadline came and passed without any progress, and Kutt was left with no other option but to openly confront the guarantors during a general shareholders' meeting.

A revolution of his own

With the guarantors unwilling to ease their financial grip on MCM and the Kutt/MCM Agreement discussions stalled, Kutt decided to win his managerial powers back on a new battlefield: corporate governance. What he had in mind was to amend MCM By-law No. 1, which specified, among many other things, the way the officers of the corporation were elected, charged with responsibilities, and removed from office. This by-law had

already been amended once on 16 July, paving the way for the
board of directors to relieve Kutt from his principal managerial
responsibilities. It is not surprising, therefore, that Kutt's proposed amendment to the by-law would be a major shift of corporate power from the board to shareholders and the president:
all of MCM's officers, including the president, were to be elected
yearly by the shareholders of the corporation at a general meeting and would not be appointed or elected in any other manner.
The president had to be a board member and no board decision
or action was to be effective unless all the directors consented
to it in writing. This would give the president veto power, and
the presidential corporate powers, as specified by Kutt in the
amended by-law, were vast:

> The president shall, when present, preside at all meetings
> of the shareholders and of the board and shall be charged
> with the general supervision of the business and affairs
> of the corporation. Except when a general manager or
> a managing director has been elected or appointed, the
> president shall also have the powers and be charged with
> the duties of that office.

On 24 September, Kutt and Sandra Pannell requested that a
meeting of the board of directors be called to consider and pass
the amendment in question. In addition, they requested that the
board call a general meeting of MCM's shareholders to elect the
company's officers in accordance with the amended By-law No.
1 and to consider removing Wallace from the board of directors
and replacing him with Laraya. That was a full frontal attack
on the guarantors. Because of Kutt and Pannell's majority share
holding position, their request to hold a meeting had to be
granted by the board in accordance with the Canada Business
Corporation Act.

Clearly, Kutt did not expect the board to suddenly submit to his demands and to reinstate a strong presidential office because of the threat of a shareholders' revolt against the guarantors, at least not at this point. Indeed, a week later, during the 1 October board of directors' meeting, Robertson, as a counsel to the company, advised against passing Kutt's amendment to By-law No 1. In his view, such an amendment, if passed, would amount to transferring the powers of the board of directors to the president alone and "appeared to constitute an abdication of their duty to manage the affairs of the Company." He recommended that the directors take a stalling approach to Kutt and Pannell's request and consider the matter at the last possible day on which it could meet, pursuant to the requisition under Section 101(1) of the Business Corporation Act.

Robertson's delaying tactic prompted Kutt to go over the directors' heads and approach the shareholders directly. He would call a shareholders' meeting, use his controlling shares to pass the amendment, and finally elect himself as president. To give muscle to the shareholders' support for his plan, he mailed a dramatic five-page long letter to the shareholders dated 18 October 1974.

Dear Shareholder:

You will find enclosed herewith a notice of a meeting of the shareholders of Micro Computer Machines Inc. called by me and to be held on October 29, 1974 ...

The meeting has been called by me to pass the draft By-law ... to elect officers. If passed, the By-law would have the following effects:

(1) All officers of the company would be elected by the shareholders and would not be appointed by the directors ...

(2) The president's powers are broadened in that he has concurrent authority with the directors in the delegation of duties to Vice-Presidents, the control of the General Manager, and fixing the duties and responsibilities of other officers.

(3) The directors of the company are prohibited from allotting or issuing any common shares unless the same are first offered to the then shareholders of the Company for subscription ...

(4) No resolution of the board is to be effective unless it is set forth in writing and consented to by the signatures of all of the directors of the Company.

It is to be emphasized that this meeting has been called by me not in my capacity as the President or a director of the Company, but in my capacity as a shareholder of the Company.

In his letter, Kutt did not hide his objectives of creating a powerful presidential office and of using his shares to vote himself into such an office. "At the forthcoming shareholders' meeting I intend to vote all of my shares to pass the proposed By-law," declared Kutt, "and, if the same is passed, to elect myself as President of the Company. The result will be that I will be able to carry on the day to day management of the Company."

Kutt's 18 October letter to the shareholders was more than just a formal call for a meeting and a detailed description of the proposed amendment to By-law No. 1. It was a dramatic appeal to support his rescue package for MCM, which was based on corporate reforms and transparency, on shareholders gaining more control over corporate affairs, and, finally, on Kutt's new plan to raise enough funds to take MCM off the receivership path and to begin full-scale manufacturing of the MCM/70.

Kutt began his plea for the shareholders' support with his account of the events at MCM which, in his opinion, had led to prolonged corporate unrest and to his decision to call upon shareholders to clean up the house. He mentioned the dissatisfaction of the management personnel with the way the company was managed, which had led to the board of directors' 16 July decision to drastically limit the presidential role in managing the company. He also wrote about the board of directors' rather irresponsible position with respect to the power supply crises and the financial situation of the company.

> Early in March of this year [1974] I had proposed to the board, with the support at that time of the senior staff of the Company, that salaries be reduced and that other measures be taken so as to conserve the available cash resources of the Company. The board in its wisdom refused to act on my recommendation, although it did allow me to cease drawing my own salary.
>
> After my powers were limited the operating expenses of the Company increased from approximately $40,000 per month to approximately $49,000 per month. As well, in my view, no real progress was made in the manufacture of our product.

By 1 October, reported Kutt, "Cash on hand and in the bank amounted to less than $8,000 and the remaining available bank line was less than $50,000." These financial strictures had to result in the layoffs announced on 2 October.

In his letter, Kutt implicitly accused Wallace, Robertson, and Elliot of not acting in the best interest of the company at such a critical moment. He reported that Wallace authorized a $10,000 payment to Borden & Elliot on account of their fees as counsel to MCM. "I objected strongly to Mr. Wallace," reported Kutt, "because both W. Struan Robertson and B.V. Elliot, partners of the firm, had assured me that the Company would not have to pay Borden & Elliot until such time as it could afford to do so."

Finally, with total disregard for shareholders with high blood pressure, he shared his deepest concern that the guarantors' possible preparation for a complete takeover of MCM would have potentially negative implications for many current MCM shareholders. According to Kutt, he was advised on earlier occasions by Robertson of the guarantors' concern over the financial position of MCM:

> It has been intimated to me that the guarantors may attempt to induce the [Toronto Dominion] bank to call its loan. I have been told by Mr. Robertson that in such event the guarantors might under their guarantee redeem the loan (thereby acquiring the right to the security granted to the bank for the repayment of the loan) and that in such event the guarantors might form another company to purchase the Company's assets and undertaking in satisfaction of the Company's bank indebtedness.

In such an event, neither Kutt nor any other shareholder would acquire any interest in the new company, except to the extent granted by the new company. "I am most alarmed to learn," continued Kutt, "that Mr. Robertson has just resigned as a director of the Company and that Borden & Elliot have just resigned as the solicitors for the Company, both citing potential conflicts of interest."

In the letter, Kutt proposed a plan for raising additional funds. "[During the shareholders' meeting,] I intend to propose that all of the shareholders of the Company provide additional financing to the Company by way of a secured loan ... As an interim measure I have indicated to the Company that I would be prepared to advance on the same basis up to $50,000." Through the October layoffs and other cost reduction measures, MCM's operating expenses were reduced to approximately $23,000 per month. Kutt concluded that "the $50,000 financing which I'm willing to provide together with the available bank line will be adequate for the Company's needs until such times as other financing arrangements have been settled."

The letter had been sent out. Now, he could only wait. If he could just hold on until the 29 October shareholders' meeting, he would vote himself back to power, the MCM/70 would start shipping in quantities, and his entrepreneurial ambitions to bring the world's first personal computer to market could finally be realized. But that was unlikely. The successful execution of even logically proven plans can be guaranteed only in the absence of countermeasures deployed by one's adversaries. Robertson's recent resignation from the board of directors and Borden & Elliot's disassociation from MCM were just the first signs of things to come.

Kutt's last stand

In a sudden turn of events, Kutt finally succeeded in convincing the board of directors to restore his corporate authorities. He arrived at the 21 October board meeting, the last meeting of directors before the 29 October showdown with shareholders, well prepared. He was accompanied by Laraya and Rea, whose support he had secured earlier during an informal get-together at his house in Willowdale. Recollecting the Willowdale meeting, Rea stressed Kutt's determination to regain control of MCM. "He was going to take back the company. He said that he would concentrate on finances and marketing ... I would be something like vice-president of operations or executive vice-president, or something like that ... looking after all the day-to-day stuff: manufacturing, engineering; I guess even the software group would be under this executive vice-president level. José would become vice-president of engineering which José really wanted all along." To gain their support, continued Rea, "he

Reg Rea operating an MCM/70 in 2005. (Source: York University
Computer Museum, photograph by Z. Stachniak.)

buttered us up saying that I did such a great job with operations
in Kingston and José was a great engineer, this and that, so,
we figured, there is nothing to lose, nothing was happening ...
Nobody was strong enough to take control and give the team
direction, we were still infighting ... So, José and I went along
with it on that basis."

During the 21 October meeting, Kutt tabled a surprising financial rescue plan for MCM. It was based on a deal he had
struck with some MCM employees (Rea, Laraya, Rivington,
Arpin, and Swanson). The proposed plan was the $175,000
loan to MCM, consisting of a $120,000 cash component and
$55,000 in salary waivers for a specified period of time. To
make this possible, Kutt wanted all the by-laws passed on 16
July 1974, which started the devastating power struggle, to be
rescinded. Wallace was to resign as managing director of MCM
and Kutt was to be fully reinstated as president and CEO of
MCM with all the necessary authority to execute his managerial
duties effectively.

This wasn't the first financial proposal Kutt had devised to help the cash-starved MCM and to regain his control of MCM. During an earlier board meeting, on 1 October, he had informed the directors that he was expecting to have financial arrangements completed very shortly that would result in up to $300,000 of new capital being invested in MCM on the condition that "he be restored to the position of full authority as President." The board agreed that every effort should be made to avoid falling into receivership, including giving full consideration to Kutt's arrangement for the new investment. Robertson stated that representatives of the guarantors had met with the proposed new investors, John T. Chittick and Manny Y. Rotman, and that it appeared likely that satisfactory arrangements could be made with the guarantors so that the bank loan would not be called immediately if the new investment were made.

But the deal with Chittick and Rotman didn't go through. The legal documents drawn up by Robertson were completely unsatisfactory to the potential new investors because of "the unacceptable position in which they placed Kutt." In short, Kutt was to remain a powerless president. Robertson's proposed agreement with the new investors also called for Kutt to withdraw his request to amend By-law No. 1 and to cancel the general meeting of shareholders scheduled for 29 October. Furthermore, the potential investors' insistence that the current guarantors of the bank loan formally agree to support the existing bank line "without any legal 'hassles'" was unacceptable to the guarantors.

So, it wasn't the deal with Chittick and Rotman that propelled Kutt back to power, but the new proposal based on individual loans and salary waivers tabled by Kutt on 21 October. The reaction of the directors to Kutt's latest financial rescue plan was positive. Michael Davis argued in support of Kutt's offer, calling it a last-ditch rescue attempt. All the directors (except Robertson, who had resigned his position a few days earlier) agreed to take the necessary steps to implement their part of the new agreement with Kutt. However, Wallace and Thomson indicated that they would also resign as directors as soon as this agreement was signed. A long-awaited triumph for Kutt, at last! Now, Kutt was only days away from the 29 October shareholders' meeting that would cement his victory.

Waiting for the shareholders meeting, Kutt could only speculate what actions, if any, would be taken by the guarantors in response to the latest events. When asked about a possible action by the Borden & Elliot Group that could cause the Toronto Dominion Bank loan to be called, Kutt could only express his doubt that any director, present or past, would willingly cause such action since "he would not be acting in the best interest of the Company, as required by law."

He didn't need to wait long. Five days before the critical shareholders' meeting, Kutt was asked to meet with Elliot on 25 October at Borden & Elliot's Toronto office located on University Avenue. It is not clear what Kutt's expectations were as to the outcome of that meeting. Armed with the board of directors' support for his new financial plan for MCM, he perhaps hoped to secure a financial commitment from the guarantors to further support the bank loan. Rea, who in an interview for this book described the events of the last few weeks as Kutt's "reversed cue," remembered vividly Kutt's preparations for the decisive meeting with Elliot. "Mers called and said 'I'm meeting with the board at … [the Borden & Elliot] lawyers' office … I want you boys to come down, be available, if I need you for support … I'm gonna make a play through the board [for] getting the company back.' So José [Laraya] and I went down [to Toronto] and met with him in the morning. And then he said 'I'm just going over [to Borden & Elliot].'"

Kutt entered the meeting room of Borden & Elliot. Elliot and others were waiting for him. And then it began. "They put

the boots to me," protested Kutt. "Everything we negotiated
... they shut the window." As Kutt recollected these events, he
was told that the Toronto Dominion Bank manager handling
the MCM file had informed the guarantors about his decision
to call the bank loan. Kutt knew what that meant. He himself
had described the possible implications of such an event in his
18 October letter to the shareholders. The guarantors would
most likely convert whatever was left of MCM into a new company, and it would be up to them whether Kutt's shares would
be worth anything. Of course, starting a new company to
manufacture the MCM/70 after MCM's collapse would be expensive and risky. Legal actions by MCM shareholders might
follow, and deals with distributors, carefully negotiated by
MCM, could collapse as well. The name "MCM/70" might also
require changing to disassociate the product from the name of
a bankrupt company, and that could lead to serious marketing problems; after all, MCM had expended a lot of marketing
effort and financial resources to make its APL computer known
worldwide. In short, it would be much easier to take over MCM
just by buying Kutt out.

According to Kutt, he was presented with an ultimatum:
either he must sell his controlling shares to Elliot, or MCM
would go bankrupt and he would end up with nothing. He
was given a copy of an agreement in principle between himself
and Beverley V. Elliot, the gist of which was that he was to sell
100,000 of his MCM common shares to Elliot, effectively losing
his majority shareholding status. He signed. With his signature
on the dotted line, his "reversed cue" was over, he was history,
and his dream of bringing the world's first portable personal
microcomputer to the market was in the hands of others.

Unfortunately, no written minutes of the 25 October meeting
are available (if any were ever taken). Furthermore, Kutt's account of the events on which this part of the narrative is based
could not be independently confirmed. Instead, what we are left

with is a single-voice narrative of Mers Kutt, full of frustration and hopelessness. Kutt confessed:

> Forever etched in my mind is the picture of ... Elliot, without a concern, in front of all of us, as he walked to the telephone and called the ... bank executive ... and instructed him to drop the receivership action against MCM. In short, I succumbed to their offer to buy me out for pennies on a dollar at $150,000 because they "blackmailed" me. There is no more accurate word because they knew I would not leave the company under any other circumstances; I did not want the company to go through a receivership. They had already triggered receivership action against the company with the bank.

Kutt was devastated.

In the meantime, Rea and Laraya were waiting for Kutt in a nearby hotel, hoping that Kutt would show up smiling at any moment. "We stayed in a hotel there off Queen Street and drank coffee all day and waited, waited, waited," recollected Rea. It was a long wait, during which they might have discussed the recent layoffs at MCM that saw a number of people in Toronto and Kingston packing their belongings into cardboard boxes and leaving. During the 1 October board of directors meeting, Kutt had reported that the amount of money left in cash and on the bank loan account was barely sufficient for even one month of operations. Kutt concluded that layoffs were inevitable and urged the board to lay off most of the employees (including some senior staff) immediately, leaving four or five people involved in manufacturing. In response, Robertson suggested that it was inadvisable to act so hastily in view of the agreement with new investors (Chittick and Rotman) that would be most likely be completed within a few days, bringing new funds. He suggested delaying the decision for a few days. He pointed out that reducing MCM to less than a skeleton operation could seriously erode trust in the soundness of the MCM business and, as a result, the guarantors and the bank would be forced to take necessary action to protect their security. After heated discussion, the board resolved (with Wallace and Robertson voting against) that six people at MCM's Toronto office and one in Kingston (among them Day, Edwards, Smyth, and Wolfe) be laid off, with the announcement being delayed until Wednesday 2 October, in order to determine first whether the agreement with new investors could be reached. An additional six people were to be let go in the second round, including Genner.

It was getting late, but Rea and Laraya were still drinking coffee and waiting for Kutt. "It was six o'clock or so," said Rea. "He finally comes back and says to José and I: 'I'm sorry boys, I've lost.' He said 'I had to sell [my] shares in the company.' ... José and I were really saddened too."

According to the signed agreement, Kutt was to sell 100,000 of his common shares to Beverly V. Elliot for $150,000. His remaining shares were also taken care of in the agreement: Kutt was to deposit all shares "which he owns from time to time with the voting trustees [named in the document as Elliot, Robertson, and Richard Meech, all from Borden & Elliot] by registering such shares in their names as voting trustees and the voting trustees have sole and absolute voting powers with respect to the shares." But that was not all. Kutt was requested to sign a non-competition covenant, according to which he would stay away until 30 October 1976 from any direct or indirect business activities that could result in the manufacturing of a computer competitive (in terms of sales price and capability) with the MCM/70 or with a new computer – the MCM/77 – that MCM wanted to develop.

Finally, according to a memorandum entitled "Re: Settlement of dispute between Merslau Kutt and Borden & Elliot" and sent to Kutt, at the completion of the sale of his shares to Elliot on 30 October, Kutt was to deliver to Borden & Elliot a written apology addressed to all shareholders of Micro Computer Machines Inc. and signed by him. The details of the apology statement were to be worked out between Borden & Elliot and Richard Bain, Kutt's new counsel. A draft of the statement prepared for Kutt in the form of a letter to MCM shareholders, read

> Dear Shareholder,
> ... In my [18 October 1974] letter to you I may have implied that Borden & Elliot had not acted in the best interest of the Company. I regret any such implication. W. Struan Robertson has always acted fairly as have the other partners of Borden & Elliot, and I apologize to them if any inferences to the contrary were drawn from my letter.

In the statement, Kutt also informed the shareholders about his resignation as MCM's president and said that the guarantors intended to invest substantial additional funds in MCM to finance the successful development and marketing of MCM products. This was his last communication with the shareholders as the president of MCM. And then he was gone.

Horned angels of hard-pressed entrepreneurs

"The horned angels of hard-pressed entrepreneurs" – that's how David Thomas described some of the venture capital groups of the 1970s in his book *Knights of the New Technology*, published in 1983. They "provide money to young companies that are rich in prospects but short of cash," explained Thomas. "They expect, however, to get returns of 30 to 40 per cent a year on their investments and often demand control of ownership and management. If the entrepreneur fails to deliver on his promises of high profits, they force him out."[1]

Automatic Electronic Systems AES-90. (Source: Canada Science and Technology Museum, photograph by Z. Stachniak.)

At the time when Kutt was being outpowered and outmanoeuvred by the guarantors, another president of a Canadian electronics start-up company was going through the "Kutt scenario," fighting venture capitalists for control of his own exciting new enterprise. In 1972, Stephen Dorsey's Automatic Electronic Systems (AES), located in Montreal, introduced the world's first all-in-one programmable word processor. The AES-90 processor not only had its own screen and a comfortable keyboard but was also able to store texts on, and retrieve them from, magnetic disks. Thanks to its programmability, the AES-90 word processor could be easily upgraded by just reprogramming some of the machine's ROM chips. Just a few years after the AES-90's introduction, the office equipment market would be flooded by similar products from companies all over the world.

In his book, Thomas described the step-by-step process of a venture capital group taking AES over.

AES found a lease financier in a subsidiary of the Royal Bank of Canada called RoyMarine Leasing ... [While orders for AES-90 processors were piling up] the Royal Bank decided to nix the leasing deal ... [T]he bank had

little confidence that a small company operating in Montreal could successfully stake out a place in the computer
market. Just weeks after refusing AES access to lease
financing, the Royal Bank walked in with a receiver and
took over the management from Dorsey, threatening to
force bankruptcy upon him.

Out of financial desperation, Dorsey decided to look for venture
capital and found a potential investor by the name of Innocean
Investments, owned by the Canada Development Corporation
and a group of banks. According to Thomas, Innocean behaved
more like a "vulture capitalist, waiting for its wounded prey to
die before swooping down for an easy meal." In an interview
for Thomas' book, Dorsey said that he was convinced that "Innocean just waited for us to go broke so that they could buy at
a bargain basement price instead of coming in earlier when the
company was still viable." And indeed, when things got really
bad at AES, Innocean became suddenly interested in investing
enough funds in AES to cover the company's debt to the Royal
Bank. Dorsey was offered no share in the ownership or management of AES. "Innocean called me in on a Friday and they had
a whole thing for me to sign right away," explained Dorsey to
Thomas. "It gave me zero equity. Even though the banks were
pressuring me to make a deal at any cost, and probably could
have forced me to do it, I just said. 'No deal.'"
     After Innocean offered Dorsey 25 per cent equity in the com-
pany, he signed. Like Kutt, he became the nominal president,
shadowed by a Bruce Wallace–like appointed manager. Eventually, things got so bad at AES that Dorsey was paid $135,000 to
quit the company. "Innocean wanted Dorsey to sign a promise
that he would not start a competing business," wrote Thomas,
but Dorsey refused. "I said that if I wasn't good enough to run
AES they shouldn't be afraid of me when they had Xerox, IBM,
and everybody else to contend with." Soon after, in early 1975,

Dorsey incorporated Micom Data Systems, which manufactured a successful line of Micom digital word processors and
was eventually sold to Philips.

The circumstances at MCM and AES which led to their found-
ers' leaving their respective companies under pressure from
venture capital groups were certainly different. But doesn't the
Dorsey versus Innocean case show that Kutt (using his own
words) still had a fighting position? that on 25 October he could
have salvaged more than just some portion of his investment in
MCM? Was $150,000 received from Elliot for his shares worth
giving up the idea of starting MCM International or some other
computer company to manufacture PCs? After all, MCM was
not too keen on building another computer around a microprocessor, while Kutt, Laraya, and others at MCM were strongly
convinced that microprocessor-based hardware was the future
of the computer industry. Within a year, Kutt could have had
a PC more advanced than the MCM/70 and without many of
the expensive and complex hardware features introduced to
the MCM/70 to compensate for the slow speed and rudimentary architecture of the 8008 microprocessor. The use of a new
8-bit microprocessor would have eliminated the need for virtual
memory and allowed the use of floppy drives for external storage instead of slow cassette drives employed in the MCM/70.

Finally, he could have protected his rights to manufacture
non-APL computers; both Laraya and Rea were proponents of
the BASIC programming language. In the 1970s, the BASIC programming language, developed by John Kemeny and Thomas
Kurtz at Dartmouth College in the early 1960s, was becoming
one of the software standards accepted by both the small systems industry and individual users. Although BASIC was dismissed by some as an inconsequential little programming toy,
and was even considered harmful by others, it was unquestion-
ably becoming widely popular; it was easy to learn, easy to use,

and made writing an interpreter for a microprocessor a much easier task than writing MCM/APL. In fact, in early 1974, one of MCM's part-time employees, under Rea's supervision, offered to write such an interpreter for the MCM/70. But the APL priesthood at MCM would never agree to infect the MCM/70 with a language like BASIC and the proposal was rejected. Instead, about a year later, two young software enthusiasts, Bill Gates and Paul Allen, started to write their BASIC interpreter for an Intel 8080–based hobby computer called the Altair 8800, manufactured by Micro Instrumentation and Telemetry Systems (MITS) located in Albuquerque, New Mexico. The success of their project launched Microsoft.

On 30 October 1974, Kutt left MCM for good. The world of computing would not hear from him until 1988 when he re-emerged with his new invention called the Charge Card, a little circuit board designed to speed up the operations of personal computers. Although the Charge Card was awarded *PC Magazine's* Annual Award for Technical Excellence in 1988, it never attracted attention from major PC manufacturers.

7

The Day After

For MCM, the ramifications of Kutt's departure were difficult to predict. On the one hand, the power struggle was over and the first MCM/70 computers equipped with ordinary power supplies had begun to leave the manufacturing plant in Kingston en route to distributors in Canada and the United States. Furthermore, the development of the MCM/700 – a cleaned-up version of the model /70 – was under way. On the other hand, the company's financial situation was desperate, its workforce wounded by the events of 1974 and reduced by resignations and layoffs. And, most devastating of all, with the departure of Kutt the company had lost a visionary and a dedicated entrepreneur whose understanding of the computer and electronics industries, and of the educational and consumer markets, was unrivalled at MCM. Soon, the company would be facing a powerful competitor – IBM – and Kutt's experience and intimate knowledge of IBM's marketing and corporate culture could have at least partially compensated for MCM's scarce marketing resources. But he was never to return.

MCM needed a new corporate leader who, in the short term, would quickly re-structure the company's operations to increase the MCM/70's sales to a level that would bring some financial stability to the company. In the long term, Kutt's successor would need to build a research and development infrastructure

Theodore (Ted) Berg.
(Source: MCM *News* 1, no.
1 [1975].)

capable of delivering a new generation of competitive products to expand the company's share of the small business computer market. The company's managing director, Bruce Wallace, had neither the entrepreneurial experience, knowledge, nor leadership skills to lead MCM. It was not until May 1975 that MCM's presidency was offered to Theodore (Ted) Berg.

President Berg

Before joining MCM, Ted Berg was a vice-president of ILC Data Device Corporation (DDC) of Hicksville, New York, a company specializing in data interface products. In early 1974, MCM appointed DDC as the exclusive distributor of MCM computers to scientific and technical markets in the United States. Berg was directly involved in the MCM partnership and was one of a very few individuals outside MCM with a solid knowledge of the MCM/70 project and a fair understanding of the difficulties that MCM was facing. Already in July 1974, Berg had offered to help MCM to overcome its organizational difficulties and to salvage the MCM/70. In spite of the high "mortality rate" of the MCM/70 demonstration units at DDC, due mostly to power supply problems, he was confident that the personal computer concept represented by the MCM/70 signaled a new era in affordable computing. He was sure the MCM computer would create a vast and lucrative market niche for itself and similar hardware. On the notorious power supply issue, Berg shared the opinion of Kutt, Laraya, and Rea that the success of the MCM/70 in the marketplace did not depend critically on the degree of sophistication of its power supply.

Berg's immediate tasks as MCM's president were to increase the sales of MCM/70s and to focus the company's activities on finishing the MCM/700 refinement of the model /70. Externally, there was no difference between the /70 and /700 models; both computers used the same case, keyboard, and display. They also used the same Intel 8008 microprocessor. However, the /700 model could have as much as 32K of ROM (containing EASY, AVS, and an improved MCM/APL interpreter) and could be interfaced with a range of peripheral equipment such as the SDS-250 and DDS-500 floppy disk drives, the MCP-132 printer, the VDU-2480 and VDU-9620 external displays, the PMR-400 card reader, and a modem, all announced in the second half of 1975. The company set up the MCM *User Club* and started to publish the MCM *News* newsletter for its shareholders, distributors, and users.

MCM identified the small business systems market as the largest and potentially most profitable for its computers. The company estimated that in the United States alone there were more than a million businesses and other organizations employing fewer than 150 people. These businesses, including retail and wholesaling firms, building contractors, and manufacturing companies, were the primary targets of small business computer manufacturers. Berg knew that making inroads in this market with the MCM/700, given MCM's scarce financial resources, would be challenging. What he didn't know was that IBM's appetite for the same market was growing fast and that in less than four months into his presidency at MCM another desktop APL computer would appear, this time sporting not "MCM" but the easily recognizable IBM logo. The decisions that Berg was to make in response to the IBM challenge would be critical to the acceptance of MCM products in the marketplace, and indeed to MCM's survival.

The IBM 5100 desktop computer was announced by IBM's General Systems Division in September 1975. It was intended as a personal computing tool for applications in engineering, accounting, research, and other areas that could benefit from computer-based problem-solving tools. The computer was programmable in both BASIC and APL and was supported by three libraries of problem-solving routines. There is some anecdotal evidence that the IBM 5100 was built in response to the MCM/70 with its potential for serving the needs of small and medium-sized businesses. What is known for certain, however, is that IBM had tried to develop a small "personal" computer on at least two other occasions in the past. The mid-1960s saw the IBM 1570 workstation project, also known as "Elsie," at IBM's Los Gatos Laboratory. Then, in the early 1970s, the IBM Scientific Center in Palo Alto, California, was involved in the SCAMP APL desktop computer initiative. However, none of these early projects passed the prototype stage. The IBM 5100 was a different story: it was manufactured and sold, and IBM made sure that the APL community was well informed about it.

By the fall of 1975, Berg was alarmed to see that some magazines featured the IBM 5100 and mentioned other small systems from Wang and Hewlett-Packard, but ignored MCM, as was the case with *Infosystems*, whose IBM 5100 feature article was published in the November 1975 issue.[1] Possibly distressed with this seeming marginalization of MCM, Berg wrote an open letter to the APL community, wrapping his concerns about the impact of

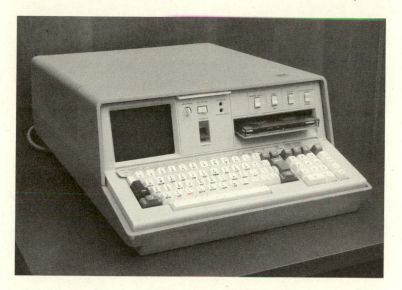

The IBM 5100 computer could be programmed in both APL and BASIC. (Source: York University Computer Museum, photograph by Z. Stachniak.)

the IBM 5100 computer on MCM operations in feigned enthusiasm for their common mission. In his letter he wrote:

Dear Friend,

I'm writing to you as a fellow member of the community of people familiar with APL, and interested in seeing more widespread use of this simple, powerful computer language ...

Until the fall of this year, we were able to call ourselves manufacturers of the only portable APL computer. Now, we can still describe our unit, the MCM/700, as the world's first and smallest.

> I refer, of course, to IBM's introduction of a desktop APL
> unit. We, at MCM, are pleased to have seen this happen.
> We feel that this will help spread the word about APL ...
> and frankly we are willing to share this burden with the
> industry's leader.

The letter seems to suggest that MCM had begun to accept the
inevitability of IBM's domination in the APL desktop computer
market and was trying to position itself as the only alternative. It
is plausible that Berg's objective was to persuade the APL community to view the future of APL desktop computing in terms
of an IBM versus MCM race, similar to other contests such as
"Coke and Pepsi, Avis and Hertz, *Newsweek* and *Time*," to
quote Owen W. Linzmayer, who came up with these analogies
to describe a similar rivalry between Apple Computer Inc. and
IBM.[2] On 24 August 1981, Apple, then a leading manufacturer
of personal computers, ran the full-page advertisement "Welcome, IBM. Seriously." in the *Wall Street Journal* in response
to IBM's announcement of its first microcomputer – the IBM
Personal Computer – which had taken place two weeks earlier.
In the ad, with staged sincerity, Apple welcomed IBM to the
world of personal computing: "We look forward to responsible
competition in the massive effort to distribute this American
[personal computer] technology to the world." By 1983, Apple's
share of the personal computer market had dropped from 23
percent in 1981 to 20 percent, while IBM's climbed sharply to
26 percent from just 18 percent a year earlier. By the mid-1990s,
Apple computers' installed base would amount to only a small
fraction of the PC world created by the IBM microcomputers
and their myriad clones.

Unfortunately, MCM was only a marginal player in the personal computer market at the time when the Apple versus IBM
contest was shaping up. One of the main factors that diminished MCM's impact on the development of personal computing

in the second half of the 1970s and early 1980s was MCM's handling of its own rivalry with IBM that had begun with the introduction of the IBM 5100 computer.

Recycling the past

By the end of 1975, MCM had sold over 150 MCM/700s and made consolidated profits of over $160,000 on sales of approximately $1.25 million. The sales forecasts for the next year were uncertain. While MCM/700 had a number of advantages over its IBM 5100 rival (the MCM computer was microprocessor-based; it was smaller, lighter, less expensive, truly portable, and featured an operating system), it was also very slow, used a dated microprocessor, and had to rely on virtual memory to compensate for its very limited amount of RAM.

MCM had to come up with a faster and more able computer to compete successfully not only with the IBM 5100 but also with scores of popular programmable calculators and desktop computers, such as the Wang 2200 family of all-in-one desktops introduced in 1973 or the Hewlett-Packard HP 9830 calculator introduced in late 1972 and programmable in a dialect of BASIC. Although programmable electronic calculators were not designed to process the payroll or customer data of a medium-scale company, their successful utilization as an efficient problem-solving tool in business, education, and engineering had continued since the introduction of Olivetti's Programma 101 desktop calculator in the mid-1960s.

Already in early 1974, MCM was researching possible directions for the development of new generation computers to replace the slow MCM/70 and maintain a safe technological distance from the competition. A year later, financially strained and no longer the leader of the pack, MCM was carefully weighing its options, looking for ways to build new hardware by reusing as much of its existing technology as possible. One of the main problems was whether the ROM chips containing the MCM/70's operating software could be reused in a new computer. For its MCM/70 project, MCM had contracted Electronic Arrays to fabricate large quantities of such ROM chips at a time when the company was still aiming at a monthly sales target of 1,000 MCM computers for 1975. However, by the end of 1974, these production targets had had to be substantially scaled down, but the ROM chips from Electronic Arrays were piling up. "Now, how do you develop a computer that would make use of these read-only memory chips, and the binary code that Gord [Ramer] and Don [Genner] had put together?" asked Laraya in an interview. "After all, it was a big [software] system that took a long time to debug." With this question, Laraya was hinting at one of the main obstacles MCM had to overcome if it wanted to re-use these ROM chips in new products: the software contained in these chips was tightly connected to the Intel 8008's architecture. In other words, the chips were meant to operate with the 8008 microprocessor, and if MCM wanted to re-use them, it had to find a way to replicate the 8008 processor. And this is exactly how MCM's new computer – the MCM/800 – was put together. The computer's central processing unit was built using a large number of TTL semiconductor devices. It was able to execute the same instruction set as the 8008 but at a much higher speed. With this design shortcut, the company was abandoning, forever as it turned out, the microprocessor technology path on which it was founded.

The MCM/800 was packaged in a new case and had an internal fan to dissipate heat – the feature so passionately discussed during the MCM/70's development. But like the /700 model, the new computer was difficult to upgrade and service.

MCM announced its new computer in July 1976 and advertised it as "the combination of data processing and word processing for as little as $400 a month." It was targeted at problem-solving and small business markets. "A typical business system

1976 promotional photograph of the MCM/800. (Source: York
University Computer Museum, photographer unknown.)

starts at $1,000 a month," explained Berg during a 1977 pres-
entation to press and industry representatives. "Our unit on a
full payout lease over five years could run about $350 a month.
We're going to try to make a computer available to small users,
or individuals who are not scientists or engineers. Anybody can
use one; even retail stores are using computers. The software
makes it possible, and APL as a high-level language. The major
advantage with APL is you don't tell the computer how to do
anything; you tell it *what* you want, not how."

In early 1974, in a document entitled *Micro Computer Machines: Development Policy*, Ramer sketched two possible de-
velopmental paths for the company. One was based on giving

up on Intel microprocessors and working with proven technologies, such as TTL, instead. The other was to continue on the microprocessor path by first adopting a more advanced Intel 8080 microprocessor. Ramer was aware that the 8080 approach would increase the computer's RAM memory and speed. Furthermore, these gains could reduce the reliance on virtual memory, first developed for the MCM/70, a memory system which was vast in capacity but slow in operation.

At the time of writing his report, Ramer was concerned with the semiconductor industry's long-term commitment to the development of new-generation microprocessors and, as a result, he was not in favour of the microprocessor direction. But by 1976, at the time of the MCM/800's development, the situation had changed entirely. Not only were more and more semiconductor companies offering their own microprocessors, but also a rapidly growing number of small and well-established companies outside of the semiconductor industry were beginning to offer complete microcomputer systems, ranging from hobby microcomputers and microprocessor development systems to full-fledged general purpose microcomputers and microprocessor-based minis. Among the established minicomputer makers, Computer Automation, General Automation, and Digital Equipment Corporation were the first to incorporate microprocessors into their products. Microprocessor-based minis were promoted as low-end and low-cost machines complementing an established line. They were designed to use the extensive software libraries available with the rest of the line. For instance, General Automation's LSI-12/16 microcomputer was built to replace the company's SPC-12 mini. The 16-bit version of the LSI-12 microcomputer was said to be functionally equivalent to the company's speedy SPC-16 mini. The CPUs of both of these microcomputers employed Rockwell International's SOS microprocessor chip set.[3] In spite of these developments, MCM decided to sacrifice its microprocessor heritage –

one of the main features that distinguished MCM products from
IBM desktops – for temporary gains of operational speed and
some reduction in development costs. The "Micro" prefix in the
company's name became void of meaning, and perhaps this is
why it was changed to "MCM Computers" in July 1977.

Technological advancements in the semiconductor industry,
which had once propelled MCM to the front line of pioneering
work on personal computing, were now bypassing the company
that was consciously turning away from what microprocessor technology had to offer. The company was losing not only
technological leadership but also key personnel, most notably
MCM's engineering icon, José Laraya. "[W]e weren't gonna do
the 8080 or 8086 [microprocessor-based hardware], we were
getting left behind," explained Laraya. "I felt that there was
nothing more to contribute." After leaving MCM, Laraya would
continue his pioneering work on personal computers. His Per-
sona desktops, designed for a Canadian company, Nelma Electronics Ltd, became popular microcomputers in Ontario in the
early 1980s.

Williams for Berg

The MCM/800 gamble ended in a fiasco. Despite re-using the
MCM/700 technology, the MCM/800 was more expensive than
its predecessor (in July 1976 the MCM/800 in basic configuration was priced at $19,800, while the top model of the MCM/700
retailed at $9,800; by July 1978, the price of the MCM/800 was
reduced to $15,000). The company managed to sell a few of its
computers to well-known firms and organizations, including the
Canadian Department of National Defence (war-game simulations), Canadian General Insurance (actuarial use), Crown Life
Insurance (actuarial and underwriting use), Ontario Hydro
(scientific use), University of Toronto (educational use), Merrill
Lynch Royal Securities Ltd (research), John Hancock Mutual

Life Insurance (actuarial use), the governments of Ontario and the Northwest Territories, and NASA.

There were some satisfied customers. "My first introduction to the MCM/800 was in 1978 when I was with Halifax Insurance," recollected Haron Ezer,

> At the time I was involved in five-year modelling plus actuarial calculations. I was using I.P. Sharp [an APL time-sharing system] to program all those tasks at very high cost.
>
> In 1978 one of Gord [Ramer]'s colleagues came to demo the MCM/800. I saw great potential with the screen and the 8-inch floppy [drives]. I felt that I could do all the actuarial formulas and the 5 year model that I had with I.P. Sharp. I convinced my boss that I could make it pay for itself within 3 months ... I actually had so many applications running on it within 3 months that it actually paid for itself 3 folds [sic].

However, by the end of 1978, only a handful of the /800 computers were installed, and there was no doubt that Berg's MCM/800 computer could not keep MCM afloat. The company's earnings plummeted from $1.25 million in 1977 to only $866,145 in 1978, almost a thirty per cent drop, with the total loss climbing to almost one and a half million dollars. Neither Berg nor any of his successors was able to come up with a winning marketing strategy for MCM products. From the very beginning of its corporate history, MCM had made the decision to sell its products through a worldwide network of distributors. Such an ambitious marketing structure required thorough market analysis, training of distributors' sales personnel, development of demonstration software, extensive national and international advertising and promotion campaigns, participation in trade shows, and production and distribution of promotional literature, brochures, data sheets, and manuals. All of these projects required marketing efforts and financial resources that MCM could never secure. "It's a case of being there first and not realizing how expensive it is to tell people what you're doing. Because that was our biggest problem," explained Ramer.

Most difficult of all, it wasn't clear how best to communicate effectively the full benefits of a dedicated small, stand-alone system from MCM, and the benefits of its APL language and virtual memory, while still claiming that the system was not a utopian electronic gadget but a useful computational tool "as easy to use as a hand-held calculator." "Every sale was really a hard thing because you are going in with something totally new, something never seen before," added Ramer. Indeed, the novelty factor can act against a new computer product, when marketing fails to provide distributors with effective tools. With time, however, the novelty of small desktop computers was starting to wear off.

Marketing problems at MCM under Berg's presidency persisted. Some former MCM employees pointed their fingers at Berg himself. "What originally intrigued me was the hundreds of responses from adverts placed in trade magazines and the lack of sales," recollected Barrie Robinson, who was with MCM from January to June 1976 as director of marketing. "Ted [Berg] was convinced it was all Peter Wolfe's fault as marketing manager. At the time I tended to agree, but as time went on I can honestly say Peter did as good a job as he was allowed to do." To add weight to his words, Robinson quoted his corporate experience: "After MCM, I built Comten who were leaders in IBM compatible front-end processors (later NCR-Comten), Sytek, and Cisco [Canada] so I reckon I am well qualified to comment on MCM's failure in the market." According to Robinson, it was Berg who should be partially blamed for MCM's inability to market its computers successfully when IBM had begun to encroach on MCM's territory. "These were the days of IBM prominence and I had already experienced the lack of understanding that senior people had for how to act in the market," commented Robinson. "Having a better mousetrap did *not* mean that your product would sell like hotcakes. Ted [Berg] thought we had a better mousetrap and people would buy them by the gross."

According to Robinson, Berg's micro-managerial style, combined with his frequent absences from MCM, was another problem. "Ted was a nice chap and good-natured, but he just was not a company builder, nor a computer salesman, nor a people-handler. I had to practically pass everything by him before I did anything!" One event that stuck vividly in Robinson's memory concerned a Chinese company that Robinson attracted to the MCM/700 computer.

> I wrote them a letter and Ted had this routine where he read every letter before it went out. He stopped mine and practically rewrote it. I was looking for another job as I was not enjoying it at MCM so I let fly at him. I said, how could he possibly write a letter in English to a Chinese chap better than someone who had been educated at one of England's finest public schools and University *and* had worked with the Chinese for five years.

On 1 March 1977 Berg stepped down as president of MCM, making room for Charles (Chuck) M. Williams, who, before joining MCM, was president and general manager of Hewlett-Packard (Canada) Ltd. Berg remained as an MCM director until 8 June 1978. When MCM closed its wholly owned United States subsidiary set up by Berg in his hometown of Nanuet, New York, he became the president of the newly created Interactive Computer Systems Inc., a dedicated MCM distributor in the eastern United States.

Dynalogic DMS8 computer was introduced in 1976. (Source: York University Computer Museum, photograph by Paul Stachniak.)

An APL machine to the end

In March 1977, Williams' presidential ride at MCM was as rough and rocky as Berg's had been almost two years earlier. The company debt was huge and a threat of yet another desktop APL computer materializing from IBM hung over MCM. Even on the Canadian scene, MCM was no longer the sole manufacturer of small computer systems. In 1976, Murray Bell's Dynalogic Corporation of Ottawa introduced its first microcomputer, the Dynalogic Microcomputer System. The Dynalogic computer used an advanced Motorola 6800 microprocessor, had two built-in disk drives for external storage of programs and data, and could be programmed in a dialect of BASIC called DynaBASIC.

In January 1978, bad news about the dismal sales of MCM computers was followed by more bad news, courtesy of IBM, which had launched an improved general-purpose APL desktop computer – the IBM 5110 – targeting the data-processing needs of small companies. IBM offered its new computer in a range of configurations with up to 64K of main memory and tape or diskette storage (up to four external diskette drives could be attached). An extensive business-oriented software library was offered, as well as two programming languages, APL and BASIC. The computer was priced between $8,475 to $15,725 depending on software and hardware configurations. According to IBM, within a week of the 5110's announcement, several hundred orders had already been received. The MCM/800 was no match for the 5110, not by any stretch of the imagination, and, once again, MCM found itself in desperate need of a new computer.

In June 1978, to combat its financial crisis, MCM passed a by-law to increase the authorized capital from $2 million to $5 million by the creation of an additional three million shares without per value. To deal with the IBM 5110 threat, MCM developed its new APL computer – the MCM/900 – in record time. The new computer, whose main architect was André Arpin, was announced in September 1978 and advertised as a minicomputer business system especially well-suited for actuarial applications. It was priced between $9,300 and $25,000 depending on configuration and presented as an alternative to expensive APL time-sharing systems. "If you spend more than $500 a month for APL time-share ... you should own an MCM System 900," reads one of the MCM/900's promotional brochures. The computer's virtual memory, claimed MCM, would satisfy the storage requirements of even mid-sized companies. In spite of its rather dull-looking packaging, the computer was reliable and, in time, was provided with a well-stocked software library developed mostly by APL Datasystems Ltd.

1978 promotional photograph of MCM's next generation MCM/900 computer. (Source: York University Computer Museum, photographer unknown.)

Like previous MCM computers, the /900 model supported the APL language exclusively. APL was a powerful programming language and, due to its spreadsheet-like features, a darling of the insurance and actuarial industries in the 1970s – the main focus of MCM marketing. In 1972, the development of an APL interpreter for the rudimentary microprocessor that the 8008

If you spend more than $500. a month for APL time-sharing ... you should own an MCM System 900.

People like Merrill Lynch, John Hancock, Ontario Hydro and Mony Life already do.
(The reasons are on the reverse)

MCM Computers Limited
6700 Finch Avenue West, Suite 600, Rexdale, Ontario M9W 5P5
a canadian computer company

MCM/900 computer marketing brochure, 1978. (Source: York University Computer Museum.)

chip was, was a challenging task that required a great deal of expertise. In the end, the MCM/APL interpreter developed for the MCM/70 was slow (a consequence of the instruction set, speed, and memory addressing limitations of the 8008), but APL's efficient syntax made the language a suitable choice for this computer and its /700 refinement.

But that was in 1972. In 1979, APL's popularity was already coming to a standstill, and MCM's commitment to APL should have been re-evaluated. Other programming languages such as BASIC, Fortran 77, C, and Pascal were still gaining in popularity, and some MCM employees were of the opinion that tying MCM products exclusively to APL was becoming a major obstacle to capturing enough of the small systems market for the company to grow. "One of the things that hurt MCM was APL.

I think that's a marvelous language," said Arpin. "But it is not the language for the masses. It is really esoteric." IBM equipped its 5100 and 5110 desktops with both APL and BASIC, and MCM could have done the same. There was some talk at MCM of supplying the MCM/800 with a BASIC interpreter at the time when the sales of the machine had almost stalled. "And one decision was," said Ramer, "well, we put BASIC on it [the MCM/800] and a word processor." But, in the end, nothing was done and MCM was unable to benefit from the growing acceptance of BASIC and other languages. Instead, the APL priesthood within MCM was utterly devoted to winning the hearts and souls of the APL community, which they perceived as the ultimate judge of MCM's endeavour. Unfortunately for MCM, APLers were largely reluctant to see the MCM machines as more than just slow, curious-looking systems that happened to run a dialect of APL. "But the APL community was not the right judge," explained Arpin. "They were not the ones that [were] gonna buy it, because they were all working on [the] I.P. Sharp [time-sharing system]. They wanted that big, big system. They were not the customers."

Whether it was in his job description or just his own strong conviction about APL's superiority, Williams also promoted MCM desktop computers as exclusively APL hardware, at all costs. "MCM had pioneered its [APL's] use in a mini during 1974," explained Williams during a 1977 presentation to press and industry representatives. "We took a gamble on it – now we've seen acceptance at all levels from students through computer professionals ... We have decided to be a specialist in APL." However, finding a strategy to successfully promote MCM as an APL company to a large and well-defined segment of the data processing market was beyond challenging. In March 1979, in an interview with *Canadian Datasystems*, Williams admitted to persistent marketing problems: "We've a spotty record in marketing. Our strength has definitely been on the technology side, and we've had problems reaching and supporting the market."[4] Williams further admitted that after more than seven years from its incorporation, the company was still looking for a market niche for its computers. "We intend to find our own special niche within the APL segment of the data processing market." He defined that market niche as the "Solution Market," whose ideal customer was a businessperson who wanted problems to be solved efficiently on his or her own computer but wasn't particularly concerned about the software and hardware technology employed to get it done. But in that case, the main pillar of MCM marketing should not have been APL but the superiority of MCM application software, competitive pricing, and service support. Instead, resorting to the corporate rhetoric worked out by his presidential predecessors at MCM, Williams talked about APL's simplicity and efficiency. "APL is a very concise language that lets you work quickly and with fewer keystrokes required. It's probably from three to 20 times as efficient as various other programming languages. It's because of such advantages that MCM has always had and continues to have such a strong dedication to the use of APL in our products." To the computer novice, APL, as characterized by Williams, must have seemed like a programming tool of startling simplicity and efficiency. That impression might not last after a would-be APLer was exposed to the language's peculiar character set and keyboard layout, or realized that the world of APL was full of incompatible dialects offered by many vendors. An experienced computer user might have pointed out deficiencies in APL's traditionally oversimplified concept of the workspace, or claimed that Williams' notion of program efficiency was misleading and that some longer programs might perform much better than short ones. But to Williams, "Drawbacks of APL, such as ... somewhat slower program-running time, are not seen as being a problem for the types of end-user requirements MCM aims to satisfy." It was clear that under Williams'

Birnam John Finch
Woods, c. 1980.
(Photograph courtesy
of B.J.F. Woods.)

presidency, if MCM were to be buried, then it would have to be
with a full APL funeral service.

Williams didn't need to defend his APL position for very long.
In December of 1979, he vacated the office of MCM president.
The new president and CEO was Birnam John Finch Woods. "I
was the physician called in by Bruce Wallace and Struan Robertson [to save MCM] when Chuck Williams bailed out," explained Woods. "Unfortunately I was unable to cure the patient
with the limited resources available and I had to officiate at the
funeral."

Woods came to MCM with considerable computer industry experience. Before MCM, he had worked for, among other firms,
Honeywell, Sperry Univac, and, very briefly, Kutt's first company, Consolidated Computer, as vice-president of marketing-
ing. At Sperry Univac he was Canadian director for the BC/7
Business-Oriented microcomputer system, which was much like
the MCM/900.
    Woods was also paying close attention to the North Amer-
ican microcomputer market. In his August 1980 article entitled

"APL makes for more powerful micros," published in *Computing Canada*, he estimated the number of manufacturers or assemblers of microcomputer-based small business systems to be in excess of 200 in the United States alone. He noted that "from a hardware point of view, at first glance there is little to differentiate one supplier from another ... A [small business] system ... may be assembled with little or no development cost by purchasing stock components and a potential computer supplier can get into business quickly with a system which seems cost competitive to a first-time user." With so many manufacturers in the marketplace, wrote Woods, "a potential user should confirm that memory expansion, hard disk capability, faster printers, and the capability for multiple operators using the system at the same time is available today – not just promised for the future ... [T]hat the system which he purchases is capable of expansion without either having his programmes rewritten or having to trade in his first system for more capacity." He pointed out that the hardware configuration of a small business system was not the only factor affecting a purchasing decision. There were other important considerations, such as the availability of extensive software libraries, of software and installation support, of continuous on-site field maintenance, and of expert advice on software packages and hardware issues pertaining to the purchaser's industry.

While Woods clearly understood how to make inroads into the small business computer market, making it happen with MCM's resources was a different thing entirely. The MCM/900 wasn't capable of supporting multiple users, and its software library included some good quality application programs but wasn't extensive. The company was downloading most of its marketing and service responsibilities to the distributors of its products. Finally, MCM's financial position was threatening the company's very survival: its $500,000 line of credit from the Toronto Dominion Bank and its government grants were

almost depleted. By the end of the 1970s, MCM was out of step
with the industry, relying on outdated bit-slice CPU technology,
and vanishing in the APL quicksand of MCM's own making.
"I could see the way things were going," commented Woods in
an interview. But he could not change everything at once. His
short-term objective was to keep the company afloat by concen-
trating on current MCM customers.

> I didn't think we were going to get too many new users.
> The biggest success that I could see was the software that
> was already established. Because people didn't really want
> to write anything new in APL. In the spring of 1980 I
> made a presentation to the Board reviewing the success of
> the past, the current evolution of the industry and a strat-
> egy for the future. Bruce Wallace commented that he was
> glad to see that someone had eventually figured out a plan
> for the future. Because before that they were in the dark as
> to what the heck is gonna happen to this company.

The board gave Woods a free hand to rescue MCM, and he came
up with the development and financing strategies to do the job.
First, he needed a new computer to replace the MCM/900. "We
made money on hardware, not software," commented Woods.
"I had to get more hardware out the door." Application software, developed outside of MCM, was seen as a tool enabling
MCM to sell more computers. What Woods wanted was simple:
to see the MCM/900 technology evolve into a multi-user, distributed data-processing network that shared peripherals and a
common file system (residing on a hard drive). The network was
planned to support up to eight work stations and to be interfaced with a large variety of peripherals. Such a system "gave
organizations a step forward as they grew," explained Woods.
The new MCM computer was announced in mid-1980. "We had
to call it something different, and 'Power' rather appealed to

The last MCM computer: the MCM Power, 1980. (Source: York University Computer Museum, photograph by Paul Stachniak.)

us," said Woods. They called a single-user, stripped-down version of the Power – the MicroPower. Looking ahead, Woods wanted to turn away from APL and bit-slice technology and enter the mainstream microcomputer field. "We were against the tide. The tide for APL and all that stuff was on its way out to the ocean somewhere to be dropped and never seen again. At that point in time, the operating system of the day was Microsoft [DOS]."

On the financial side, Woods was working on a deal with a United Kingdom–based investor group that was interested in taking over MCM. According to Woods,

> they were going to clear all the debts, buy out the shareholders and continue the company as MCM. I thought it was just fantastic. We could have generated quite a significant Canadian presence because their pockets were

MCM Power marketing brochure, 1980. (Source: York University Computer Museum.)

deep and the had the money to do that. They were quite happy with the strategic plan that I had presented, which included bringing a new 16-bit PC system to market. They had the in-house computer smarts and all that went with it. However, I told the board of MCM directors that I wasn't prepared to go ahead with this unless I had majority control.

Woods figured that once he was the majority shareholder, it would be easy to buy the remaining shares. In the end, his shares would have translated into 10 per cent shareholding in the new re-financed MCM, with the rest of the shares going to the British investor group. "A little bit devious on my part," explained Woods, "but nevertheless it was a solid recovery plan."

The board didn't resist and, as of January 1982, Woods was in possession of two-thirds of MCM common shares. "The board saw the writing on the wall and they knew if I didn't do it, they were dead anyway."

MCM made some money in 1980 – $244,000 on revenues of $1.9 million. The new MCM computers were displayed at various shows including the COMPEC'80 computer show in London, and a British firm, BL Systems Ltd, was appointed to distribute them in the United Kingdom. Then came 1981, when hardware sales stalled. Neither the MCM/900 nor the Power were able to gain the general acceptance that other personal and desktop microprocessor-powered computers, such as the small Apple][running the VisiCalc spreadsheet program, had begun to enjoy since the end of the 1970s. To make things worse, on 12 August, IBM introduced yet another desktop – the Personal Computer (PC). The speed with which the PC began to change the face of personal and office computing caught not only MCM but the majority of other microcomputer manufacturers off guard. In the not-so-distant future, most manufacturers of home and business desktop computers who could not adapt to the rapidly evolving PC world would perish. To make ends meet, MCM became a distributor for Sanyo microcomputers – a rather humbling turn of events for a company whose engineering and entrepreneurial talent had been sculpting the features of the world's first personal computers a decade earlier.

By 1982, MCM was unable to raise any new funds through bank loans or grants from either the Ontario government or the federal Department of Industry, Trade and Commerce. On 11 March, Robertson resigned as MCM's director. Then, in May, a British group of potential investors backed out. "The major stumbling block to my European investor was that at the crucial time, everyone became greedy and I was unable to negotiate what the investors considered to be a 'reasonable' buy-out cost to clear the books," said Woods. "When the financing dropped through, then I didn't have a viable company. And as a distributor of Sanyo computers, it's a different ball game. We could never pay off the debts, we could never give the return on capital," concluded Woods.

One day in late June, an MCM secretary informed Woods that some chartered accountants from Price Waterhouse were waiting for him in the MCM reception area, with orders to execute the foreclosure. He was surprised. The Toronto Dominion Bank was calling its $500,000 loan and, although rumours were rampant, none of the directors had warned him about the immanent foreclosure. On 28 June 1982, MCM terminated the offices of president and secretary and, on 30 June, it dissolved its Board of Directors. MCM's assets were auctioned off soon afterwards.

MCM's foreclosure didn't seem to register in the Ontario Ministry of Consumer and Commercial Relations files. On 15 May 1985, the ministry sent the notice of MCM's dissolution to the company's final address.

Dear Sir/Madam

NOTICE OF DISSOLUTION

Take notice that the Certificate of Incorporation/Amalgamation has been cancelled under section 240(3) of the Business Corporations Act, 1982 by an order dated 29 April 1985 and the corporation has been dissolved as of that date for default in complying with the Corporations Tax Act.

Notice of dissolution has been published in the *Ontario Gazette*.

CONCLUSIONS

■■■■■■■■

Since the 1950s, every decade or so, a new computing paradigm is introduced that profoundly changes the way we utilize computers: batch mode utilization of huge mainframe computers in the 1950s and 1960s, time-shared computing services and mini-computers in the 1960s and 70s, microcomputing in the 1970s, home and personal computing in the 1980s, and now, in the last decade, diverse forms of computer use involving laptops, net-books, tablet and slate computers, smart phones, and the emergence of cloud computing. What is the significance of the MCM efforts in the creation of our present-day digital reality? What is the MCM/70's place in the modern history of computing?

Of course, possible answers to these questions depend critically on how one measures the significance of a technological invention, especially when it is considered in the context of fast-paced innovation in high technology sectors such as the computer and semiconductor industries. To grant technological significance to an invention, one may look for a quantitative measure, such as the volume of new products manufactured as the result of an invention, or quote the amount of new employment provided by the invention-generated industry. Or, one may apply a qualitative approach and look for a direct and long-lasting impact on society, or for a chain of events leading from the invention to some profound technological, social, or cultural change.

It is rather unlikely that one can come up with a direct argument demonstrating that the MCM/70 has met, and if so, to what degree, any of these criteria. There is little but anecdotal evidence for its impact on desktop computer development at IBM in the mid-1970s. One can only conjecture that the 1973 exhibits and demonstrations of the MCM/70 and the favourable, sometimes enthusiastic, media reports on the revolutionary "Small Canadian"[1] awakened society to the real possibility of universal and affordable access to computing in the not-so-distant future. Indeed, a compact, all-in-one MCM/70 displayed next to a refrigerator-sized minicomputer during a computer show provided the first glimpse of a new computing paradigm based on individual use and ownership.

MCM was possibly the earliest company to fully recognize, articulate, and act upon the immense potential of microprocessor technology for the development of a new generation of cost-effective, individual user-oriented computing systems. The annals of MCM and the corporate histories of companies such as R2E, together with an account of the microcomputer hobbyists' movement that was to erupt at the end of 1974, paint a more complete picture of a budding personal computer industry. We see it grew from its humble beginnings, when it tried to define its purpose and open up new markets in terms of slow 8-bit machines, to its more mature state at the end of the 1970s, when the microcomputing landscape was shared by a myriad of microcomputer hardware and software manufacturers. The picture that emerges exhibits two paths originating from the same point, which was defined by the early systems activities at Intel and other semiconductor manufacturers.[2] The first path was marked out by the commercial activities of companies such as MCM and the French R2E, while the second was charted by the computer hobbyists. Both paths, mostly independent of each other, began to merge in the late 1970s when the hobby computer industry started to decline under pressure from the commercial manufacturers of desktop microcomputers and from the consumer electronics industry, which came up with a new gadget – the home computer.

To correctly assess MCM's contributions to computing, one has to scrutinize fairly the company's activities in the 1970s. Why did MCM fail to become the leader in the nascent personal computer industry, and why was the MCM/70 forgotten? Without answers to these questions, the MCM/70 narrative can never be complete.

Welcome to the computer age!

With the announcement of the MCM/70, the Canadian high technology start-up MCM was challenging the established computer industry and services with its radically different model of deploying computing technology to benefit society. New semiconductor devices made it possible to design small and affordable computers which, MCM claimed, were destined to democratize computing by expanding resources enjoyed by the largest enterprises to individual users as well as to small and medium-sized businesses. It was this unique vision of a modern society universally and freely accepting the benefits of distributed computing, a vision clearly defined and widely disseminated by MCM, that attracted considerable international attention in 1973 and swiftly elevated MCM to the position of one of the most innovative high technology companies. "There seems little doubt that Canada has stolen an early world lead in the new era of 'distributed processing' which will bring the dream of a computer in every home and office closer to reality," wrote *Electronics Communicator* following the MCM/70's announcement in Toronto.[3]

One of the earliest documents that explicitly presented MCM's position on future developments in computing and the impact of the new computer technologies on society was the company's *Media/Press Release*, dated 28 September 1973 and prepared on the occasion of the MCM/70's unveiling in Boston. The document begins with a bold declaration of a new era in computing heralded by the MCM/70's launch:

> The introduction of the world's first portable APL computer, the MCM/70, will revolutionize computer usage over the next five years ... The MCM/70 will accelerate the trend to Distributed Processing, which, in optimizing the use of data processing facilities, is the natural evolutionary course for data processing to follow.

The company's argument in support of its claims relied heavily on an analysis of the profound impact electronic handheld calculators had already had on the consumer electronics market. MCM was convinced that the speed with which its computers would gain the "must-have" personal productivity tool status would rival the unprecedented growth in popularity enjoyed by battery-operated calculators. After all, the MCM/70 looked like a desktop calculator and could even be operated on batteries – just like modern, digital pocket calculators. The MCM/70, computationally a much more powerful gadget than calculators, "could revolutionize the world of computing in the same explosive way that the hand-held calculator changed the calculator field."

The message was clear and the media liked it: "The MCM/70 ... brings to the world of computing what the $100 hand-held calculator brought to the world of calculators," wrote *Machine Design* in November 1973.[4]

The success of hand-held calculators was based on five key principles: small size, high utility, effortless operation, low cost, and personal ownership. MCM insisted that these same principles, applied to computer design, would open up new and vast application areas for computers, and that such new-generation computer systems would be irresistible to professionals, who would eventually own and routinely operate them. Of course, the MCM/70 was to burst out as that archetypal computer of the future.

> The flexibility, price and performance of the MCM/70 will set new system standards in a variety of commercial and scientific applications: office computers, satellite computers, small business or branch office information systems, data entry, scientific computers, intelligent terminals, and clusters of classroom computers.

The low cost and small size of new computer hardware could be accomplished by following in the footsteps of the calculator industry, which achieved high-degree miniaturization by using novel semiconductor devices. Furthermore, MCM was convinced that programming languages such as APL provided a solution to making computers easy to operate without sacrificing computational power and versatility. With the MCM/70 operating under APL, claimed MCM,

> complete novices will be able to begin effective computing within the first hour by following a simple "calculator type" instruction booklet which makes mockery of traditional complex programming. As a result of this simplicity, the MCM/70 will be directed at a massive market, ranging from desk top applications in [the] business, engineering, actuarial, chartered accountancy, and education fields to small and medium sized business systems.[5]

An MCM/70 owner was expected to be able to install his or her computer without any need for assistance from MCM's customer service department. MCM would supply a turnkey system, some application software, and a user manual that explained, in simple language, the principles of APL programming and everything else needed for the computer's operation.

Instead of the traditional systems engineering and programming support provided to mainframe computer users, there was MCM's encouraging message, "Good luck, and welcome to the computer age!"[6]

In sum, on 25 September 1973 in Toronto and 28 September in Boston, MCM not only unveiled a small, inexpensive, versatile, and easy-to-use personal computer, but also heralded a new era in computing based on the social acceptance of the new computing paradigm represented by hardware such as the MCM/70.

> Mr. Kutt strongly believes that in the coming years, the computer field is going to be made up of millions of small computers and a limited number of large computers, each of the small systems specializing in the jobs they do best. With this trend developing, the MCM/70 could, in a few years, become as familiar as calculators are today.

Any major technological breakthrough or scientific discovery inspires utopian sentiments. It is likely that Kutt's grand vision for future computing was received with a measure of skepticism. In the past, the advent of steam power, electricity, electronics, and even the Internet, had inspired ungrounded proclamations of a techno-panacea leading to technology-based higher forms of social liberation. But as with his vision of computing without punch cards, Kutt's analysis of computing's development, republished all over North America, was right on the mark. Or, should I say, *almost* on the mark, as the 1973 publicity was the MCM/70's first and only brush with fame.

The MCM/70 personal computer

At the time of Kutt Systems' incorporation, the computer industry did not manufacture any digital, electronic computers specifically for personal use, and the term "personal computer" wasn't in use either. The situation was different in the calculator field. In the nineteenth century, small, inexpensive, mechanical calculating machines quickly began to penetrate the market, offering rapid and reliable means of performing basic arithmetic operations to businesses.[7] Marketing of these early calculators required a language of purpose and benefits understood by every businessman. By the end of the nineteenth century, this language spoke of the calculators' operational power, simplicity of use, affordability, and private, individual ownership. In 1893, Ribbon Adder of New York was advertising its new calculating machine as one that

> does all that can be done by arithmetic – multiplying, adding, and subtracting sterling currency as well as decimal, and fractions. Simple as a tape measure, its workings are understood at a glance ... And while the prices of calculating machines hitherto have been almost prohibitive, the Ribbon Adder is furnished at a price which brings it within the means of all.[8]

These versatile mechanical calculators acquired the adjectives "personal," "pocket," and "home" in the early twentieth century. In 1904, Automatic Adding Machine Manufacturing of New York began advertising its small GEM calculator as "Your Personal Adding Machine; For Desk, Pocket, Home." Since then, the names of calculators have been frequently prefixed with "personal." The small mechanical slide adder Valiant Personal Calculator and Casio's hand-held electronic calculator named the "personal mini," can serve as examples.

Between 1973 and 1975, therefore, MCM took advantage of a century-old calculator marketing culture, basing its promotional language on the success of electronic calculators and on the failure of the computer industry and services to provide af-

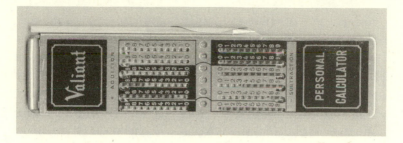

Valiant Personal Calculator. (Source: York University Computer Museum, image by Z. Stachniak.)

fordable computing to the public. The MCM/70's role was to bridge the simplicity of pocket calculators' use and the computational power of large digital electronic computers. According to MCM, its computer was

> the first complete stand-alone micro computer to provide full scale information processing capability – with the power of a large-scale computer and the ease of a programmable calculator. Right at your own desk ... or anywhere else it may be needed. At a price you can afford.[9]

The key to the MCM/70's operational simplicity was the use of the APL language and of the AVS/EASY operating system. A few simple programming examples included in the MCM/70's manuals were to convince a user of the simplicity of APL's programming. "You have now programmed a computer! Simple, wasn't it?"[10] But APL wasn't really simple, and MCM never admitted that tying its fortunes to APL exclusively was one of the main reasons why the company failed to secure a sizable market share throughout its corporate history.

Although MCM had never explicitly used the term "personal computer" in relation to the MCM/70 (it preferred to call it a "portable APL computer," a "total, stand-alone personal information processing system,"[11] or, sporadically, a "personalized computer"), the company was the first to promote commercially a microprocessor-based computer designed specifically for personal use. In 1973, in the marketing language of early mechanical calculators, MCM promoted its computer as having such "size, price, and ease-of-use as to bring personal computer ownership to business, education, and scientific users."[12] The MCM/70's promotional literature and manuals talked about individual, private, or personal computing experience: "be your own programmer," "develop your own information processing library," "become more cost-effective," "ensure full security of confidential data," and "enjoy portable hands-on information processing."[13]

The general public was to gain access to computing through personal ownership of affordable computers. According to Michael Day, who authored the MCM/70 *Introductory Manual*,

> It has been a combination of the complexity of the large computer machines and the complexity of the special computer languages, that has till now prevented the general public from using computers themselves. But the simplicity of the MCM/70 and its associated computer language (known as APL) make personal computer use and ownership a reality.[14]

The MCM/70 was an archetypal personal computer. Microprocessor-based and equipped with semiconductor memory, it was intended for individual use and, possibly, ownership (in 1974, even the basic model of the MCM/70, with a price tag of $3,500, was prohibitively expensive for an average individual). Like laptops and desktops of today, it was a general-purpose computer running under an operating system designed to provide an effortless interaction with the computer.

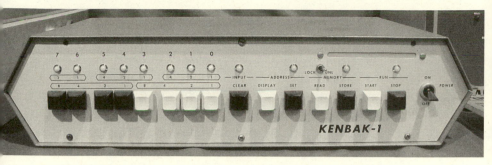

Kenbak-1 educational computer. (Photograph by Z. Stachniak.)

Of course, computers were being manufactured for personal ownership and use long before the MCM/70's announcement. But these were simple educational devices, such as Berkeley's relay-based Simon or the digital, electronic Kenbak-1 computer sold by Kenbak Corporation in 1971. Even the promotional language used by Kenbak resembled that adopted two years later by MCM. "Modern electronic technology created the Kenbak-1 with prices that even private individuals and small schools can afford," read a 1971 ad placed by Kenbak in the *Scientific American.* "Very quickly you, or your family or students, can write programs of fun and interest."[15] But with just 256 bytes of memory and no microprocessor, the Kenbak-1 was just another educational toy which, at the price of $750, did not find too many takers. The French Micral was not a personal computer either. This microprocessor-based computer was announced by R2E three months before the MCM/70's first public demonstration. However, the Micral was a special-purpose computer intended for, among other applications, process control, teletransmission, and the operation of scientific instrumentation. That leads us to the conclusion that the MCM/70, first demonstrated in May 1973, was possibly the earliest versatile microprocessor-based computer intended for individual use and ownership.

None of the preserved MCM corporate documents provides sufficient data to estimate how well the MCM's message of micro-computer-based distributed computing was received by the computer industry and services. One of the internal MCM documents that survived the company's closure in 1982 lists several installations of the MCM/70 in renowned financial, research, educational, and governmental institutions across North America. But such a listing of prominent corporate names is not a substitute for primary evidence of impact, and one is left only with anecdotal evidence. New York Life Insurance Company (NYLIC) – one of the largest life insurers in the world – purchased several MCM/70s. NYLIC contracted another company, Warner Computer Systems, for programming and time-sharing services. Glenn Schneider was one of the Warner Computer Systems employees charged with the evaluation of desktop and portable computer concepts such as the MCM/70 and the IBM 5100. He was also using NYLIC's MCM/70s to teach APL classes to the company's management information personnel. Twenty-five years later, Schneider recollected his exposure to the 22-pound APL computer from MCM this way: "having a portable APL machine was such a novelty back then it was a God-send ... Lugging the MCM[/70] home on the subway in New York helped build up my muscles, as it was hardly a light-weight, but it gave me great hope (and inspiration) for the future which would yet erupt."[16]

In 1973 and 1974, thousands of people attended computer shows and APL conferences where MCM demonstrated its first computer and promoted the company's vision of personalized computing. One of the people who learned about the MCM/70 that way was American teacher Harley Courtney.

I saw an early version of the MCM/70 at the Toronto
APL conference in the spring/summer of 1975. Since I
was obsessed with APL and took a job teaching at U.S.

Army posts in Europe as of September 1975, I resolved to purchase one ASAP ... After receiving it, I spent hours a day exploring the machine's capabilities, even discovering some undocumented features that were mind-boggling to me then. I taught business statistics during the fall semester of 1976 in both Frankfurt and Giessen ... I had no problems with the computer while carrying it all over Europe ... I did enjoy using the MCM/70, and it was a beautiful piece of engineering for its time.[17]

Courtney's computer now resides at the Computer History Museum in Mountain View, California.

On the other side of the Atlantic, too, MCM computers were finding their way into businesses and research institutes across Europe, from France, where the MCM/70's sales were particularly strong, to the Soviet Union. In an August 1999 interview, Andrei Kondrashev, a co-founder of Chicago-based Lingo Allegro USA, told APL Quote Quad that the Computer Centre of the Academy of Science of the USSR had a few dozen MCM computers. Kondrashev used the academy's MCM/70s to work on his college graduation project. "I even had an MCM-70 in my home for quite a long time with APL."[18]

We could have been Apple

In a confidential letter dated 20 February 1973, and addressed to A. Carr, director of the electronics branch of the Department of Industry, Trade & Commerce, MCM wrote, "Our product is truly a breakthrough and we believe we not only have the lead time to capitalize on the revolution but also the capability of maintaining our leadership through a continuous introduction to the market, of a series of models for various diverse applications within the family of products, in relatively short intervals of time."[19]

Under favourable conditions, carrying out the plan outlined in this letter would establish MCM as an undisputed leader in the new distributed computing market. Sales of MCM/70s at the predicted rate of 500–1,000 per month would generate enough revenue to pay for the development of significant application software and for the rapid construction of MCM's new generation computers employing state-of-the-art microprocessors. But in 1974, the corporate conditions at MCM were anything but favourable. A devastating power struggle, employee unrest, and financial difficulties pushed the company to the verge of collapse. Instead of the thousands of MCM/70s planned for sales and delivery in 1974, MCM managed to sell only a hundred or so. In 1975, Berg still had time to keep MCM on the personal microcomputer track. But, instead, the company responded to the IBM 5100 threat by putting all its limited resources into the ill-fated MCM/800, implemented quickly by remaking the MCM/700 using bit-slice rather than microprocessor technology. The gamble did not pay off and MCM was pushed out to the fringes of the small systems market.

The MCM/70 promotional brochures presented the computer as a cost-effective alternative to computer time-sharing services. In 1974, large time-sharing companies, such as I.P. Sharp Associates Ltd of Toronto, charged their clients, among other fees, $8 per connect hour, 35 cents for each second of CPU time, and $1 per 3,000 characters entered. Depending on an application, a user could pay $25, $100, or more per connect hour. There was not much a client connected to such a system via dumb terminal could do in less than an hour. Therefore, assuming an average rate of $100 per connect hour, it would take only about four months at an hour a day to accumulate $9,500 in computing charges – the price of a new and fully loaded MCM/700.

This same time-sharing economics was also behind IBM's introduction of its 5100 desktop computer. But IBM also had another motivation to enter the desktop computer market. Since

the early 1970s, high-end, low-priced programmable calculators from Hewlett-Packard and Wang Laboratories had been
attracting considerable attention from individual professionals
as well as small and medium-sized businesses. Useful computational tasks could be accomplished on these machines in-house
and more cost-effectively than through logging on to time-
sharing systems. Since these programmable calculators used
dialects of the BASIC programming language, IBM equipped its
5100 computer with both APL and BASIC. MCM, on the other
hand, utterly dismissed the programmable calculator market as
well as the role BASIC had begun to play in research, business,
and education. Looking back, most former key MCM employees
agreed that ignoring BASIC was a major mistake. "APL was a
good idea," explained Genner, "but had we decided to go with
BASIC right from the start we would be world leaders now, our
name would still be up there." Laraya agreed: "We would have
been like Apple ... we would be where Apple is right now."

MCM could not be like Apple Computer since, unlike the
maker of the famous Apple][microcomputer, it was cast in
rigid and self-imposed software and hardware constraints during most of its corporate existence. Unlike the MCM/70 and
the MCM/700, the Apple][, introduced during the first West
Coast Computer Fair in San Francisco in April 1977, was truly
inexpensive and could be easily expanded by its users. By mid-
1980, Apple sold over 120,000 of these computers. BASIC most
certainly contributed to the Apple]['s popularity, as tens of
thousands of useful programs were written for it in BASIC, but
the sudden surge in the computer's sales was caused by the application software VisiCalc, written by Personal Software and
offered to the Apple][users in 1979. VisiCalc was the first electronic spreadsheet program and, for a while, it was available
only on Apple][s. For author Owen Linzmayer, "VisiCalc was
arguably the first 'killer application.' It was so compelling that
people bought [Apple] hardware just to run it. It went on to

Apple][computer with two Apple Disk][floppy drives. (Source: York University Computer Museum, photograph by Z. Stachniak.)

become one of the hottest-selling software products in the personal computer industry, selling 200,000 copies in two years."[20]

Similar spreadsheet-like features of APL made the MCM machines appealing to some insurance and actuarial businesses. However, APL was not a "killer application," and the owner of an MCM computer was still required to program his or her machine to develop applications that were not in the MCM library of business-oriented software.[21] Instead of cashing in on the popularity of VisiCalc (as done by many other microcomputer companies) MCM was going against the VisiCalc wave without a compatible product.

By the early 1980s, tens of thousands of Apple][computers had entered the educational market, contributing in large part to the computer's popularity worldwide. MCM also identified education as one of the significant areas for microcomputer use. "The

MCM/70 Desk Top computer," reads *The MCM/70 in Education* promotional brochure, "represents a breakthrough in technology of tremendous significance to education." The company even proposed the "MCM/70 Classroom" concept. In its minimal configuration, such a classroom was to be equipped with from fifteen to thirty MCM/70s for individual use by students and with three to six printers to be shared among the students. However, with a price tag of $6,500 for an MCM/700 in basic configuration (with a single cassette drive) in 1975, such MCM classrooms were not realistic. Only single computers, at best, could enter high school computer classrooms. One such computer class was run by math and computer science teacher David Borrowman at Sydenham High School in Sydenham, Ontario, about 25 kilometres north of Kingston. Recollecting his early computer education efforts, Borrowman explained:

> It began in 1970 as an after school "club" at which interested students learned computer programming using FORTRAN. They coded their work on paper sheets, I then took them into Kingston to be card-punched and then run on computers at Queen's University. The cost of that would have been prohibitive if the Queen's Director of Computing at the time hadn't been so interested in providing the opportunity at no cost to high school aged students. Turnaround time was about three days.

This all changed when the school acquired an MCM/70. The school's computer provided a very practical if somewhat limited platform.

> The limitations ... had to do with the relatively small memory, the single-line plasma display screen, and (in our case) the lack of a printer in the system. I surmounted these difficulties by issuing each student their own tape

cassette on which they stored their programmes and assignment results. They submitted their work for marking
as a paper flowchart along with the cassette which I could
then run on the machine as well as view their code and
on-screen output. While far from ideal, it fit our budget
and worked well with minimal difficulties.

In the end, MCM did not develop any comprehensive educational strategy. The educational market was of interest to the
company only as long as it fit with the overall marketing objective to present the MCM computers as a cost-effective alternative to time-sharing services. By the end of 1976, most schools
could not afford even one MCM/800 at $19,800. Fortunately
for the educational market, the following year brought inexpensive microcomputers from Apple Computer, Commodore, and
Radio Shack that made a microcomputer classroom concept a
reality for the first time.[22]

The MCM MicroPower computer was introduced by MCM to
compete against small business systems such as the Apple][Plus
and Radio Shack TRS-80 Model II, both introduced in 1979
and both equipped with, among other software, VisiCalc. To
succeed, the MicroPower, as well as its predecessors, would
have required marketing manpower, expertise, and financial
resources that MCM could never have afforded. The marketing strategy adopted by MCM from the start was to create a
worldwide web of appointed distributors. The first contracts
had already been signed in early 1974 with Office Equipment of
Canada and Unicomp Canada to represent MCM on the Canadian market, and with ILC Data Device Corporation, detailed
to cover the American market. Other distributors for Europe
and Japan were to be appointed later.
    The set-up and maintenance of such an extensive network
proved to be difficult and the problems affected sales. Distribu-

tors required coherent guidelines and strategies for presenting MCM computers as a functionally irresistible and economically viable alternative. They needed a clear language highlighting the computers' unique features and benefits to show how these outweighed the machines' disadvantages, such as, in the case of the MCM/70 and /700, low speed and single-line display. They had to be provided with directions for dealing with competition from the APL and non-APL markets. Finally, they expected MCM to showcase its technology during major computer events such as the annual National Computer Conference in the United States or SICOB in Europe. But MCM was unable to do any of that. Furthermore, the company's policy against disclosing the hardware makeup of MCM computers turned into a marketing fiasco.

One of the most significant measures of a computer system's performance is its operational speed, and that depends critically on the computer's CPU. In its MCM/70, /700, and /800 promotional literature, MCM never disclosed any CPU information for its computers. In early 1973, MCM spoke of the "advanced LSI technology" behind its MCM/70, but the company never used the term "microprocessor" nor explicitly mentioned the Intel 8008 CPU chip employed by the computer. Perhaps the secrecy was insisted on to avoid compromising the technological advantage MCM held over inevitable followers.[23] In 1974, when the MCM/70 was still in the development phase, the Intel 8008 chip was already obsolete and much inferior to Intel's new 8080 CPU device. Thus, revealing the identity of the MCM/70's CPU at that time would have been damaging. Finally, since the introduction of the /800 model, MCM had abandoned the microprocessor track altogether and the microcomputer technology that MCM had helped to pioneer could not be used as a marketing ploy even when microcomputing came of age and other manufacturers were shipping thousands of microcomputers a month.

There were some strong MCM distribution outposts, such as SYSMO S.A. of Paris, France, which by 1976 was installing around ten MCM/700 systems per month. But in the end, no distributor was able to swing a mega-sale that could make MCM a feared contender in the small systems class and help it to become another Apple Computer.

Why was the MCM/70 forgotten?

Although many MCM/70s were sold around the world between 1974 and 1976, the computer seemed to be consigned to oblivion. Why was it forgotten? To answer this question, one has to go back to 1974, the year that should have belonged to the MCM/70 but didn't. Instead, prolonged corporate turmoil effectively closed the window of opportunity that would have allowed MCM/70 to become a major force in reshaping the social status of computing.

MCM's media buzz of 1973 faded to total silence in early 1974. The company's cash flow problem put an end to advertising and promotional tours. Participation in major computer shows was cancelled as well, as were the MCM/70 field trials, such as the one scheduled for 28 March to 5 April 1974 at the Canadian government's Department of Supply and Services. Throughout the year the company had no choice but to keep a low profile. The power struggle that terminated with Kutt's dismissal was too dangerous as a media topic for a company in a fragile state and in need of some stability. In 1975, when the worst seemed to be over, the company had nothing new to offer to get its products back into the media spotlight. MCM could only watch, helpless and baffled, as the giant IBM, with its newly introduced IBM 5100 desktop APL computer, decisively encroached on the very consumer market MCM had identified for its own computers.

The MCM/70 wasn't retained in the APL movement's collective memory for long either, although MCM was founded on APL and the company remained firmly committed to the language throughout its decade-long history. Gaining acceptance for its APL portable platform from the APL community was crucial to MCM, but such support wasn't easy to get. To explain why, one has to recall that throughout most of the 1970s, the computer industry viewed centralized large computer systems as the only means by which large organizations could meet their data processing needs. The APL community, resident mostly on mainframes, supported this view, and the mainframe was the focus of most APL software development activities. Although APL had never became a dominant language for mainframes, robust and mature APL products were developed during that time and successfully used in a broad range of applications.

However, MCM was developing neither large hardware systems nor groundbreaking APL software for mainframes. The announcements of MCM computers never generated any substantial discussion on the potential of microcomputers for APL expansion into new application areas, as advocated by MCM, and MCM's APL interpreter – the first such interpreter ever developed for a microcomputer – didn't capture the attention of APLers either. Perhaps a few departures from the APL standards evident in the MCM/APL language – taken by MCM to combat the MCM/70's severe shortage of memory – were unacceptable to those APL purists who were preoccupied with advancing the language and its applications on mainframe computers. Perhaps the slow speed of the MCM/70 and the short word-length of its CPU (just 8-bit) were turning people away from APL "micro-portability"; that is, from the development of APL dialects for microcomputers. Whatever the case may be, the APL community had never paid significant attention to MCM products, or to microcomputing in general, until the late 1970s when it had became evident that small, dedicated microprocessor-based systems could deliver enough computing power to successfully run many applications at much lower per user costs than either mainframes or minicomputers. Under this new economics of computing, users began to migrate large number of applications from centralized systems to microcomputers. Unfortunately, the APL community underestimated the microcomputer challenge and was unable to adapt its tools to the personal computer (PC) environment fast enough to attract PC software developers. Compared to popular programming language environments available for PCs in the 1980s, APL interpreters were expensive, slow, and without extensive utility libraries.[24]

APL could have became a dominant language for the micro-computer if only some software company had developed an APL interpreter for early microcomputers based on popular micro-processors such as the Intel 8080 or Zilog Z80. In the 1970s, those who identified microcomputers with BASIC and viewed that language as an insignificant programming toy, could have entered the microcomputer market earlier by choosing an APL-based machine. In view of the popularity of APL, such a company could have derived substantial profits from selling its APL software – the same way Microsoft was paying its bills with the sales of BASIC. In fact it was Microsoft's co-founder and APL's vocal supporter Bill Gates who wanted to do just that. Micro-soft had been developing its own APL interpreter since 1976, perhaps under the influence of IBM's introduction of its APL-based IBM 5100 computer. "Equivalence with the 5100 was my goal," explained Gates in his March 1979 interview for *ETI Canada*.[25] After the success of Microsoft BASIC, first offered to the owners of the Altair 8800 microcomputers in mid-1975, "APL seemed like a great follow-on product," continued Gates. However, in 1976, Microsoft was still a small software com-pany carefully addressing market needs. FORTRAN got higher priority and by the end of 1976, only one person was left at Microsoft to continue the APL work. Microsoft FORTRAN was introduced in June 1977 and COBOL the following year. It was not until 1979 that Microsoft announced its APL-80 interpreter for the Intel 8080 and Zilog Z80 platforms. It was to be out in April 1979 and compatible with IBM's APL.SV software. But in the end the Microsoft APL-80 proved to be vaporware and by the early 1980s, it was Microsoft's BASIC and not APL that was installed on the majority of personal computers.

MCM was a hardware company exclusively. Selling its APL software to other computer manufacturers would have undermined the company's hardware objectives. In short, MCM could popularize APL only through successful installations of its systems; the support from the APL community would have benefited both MCM and the APL movement. But such support never materialized. It is likely that MCM failed to present its products adequately to APLers, even when opportunities to do so presented themselves.[26] However, by losing MCM – APL's strongest supporter in the small systems market – from its side, the APL movement missed a unique opportunity for allowing its language to have a real impact on the microcomputer's market formation. By leaving MCM to itself, the movement allowed APL to be written off as a dominating microcomputer language and left the rapidly growing microcomputer market almost entirely to BASIC. Although some desktop microcomputers would eventually be equipped with an APL interpreter,[27] the language would never become a major programming tool on the microcomputer platform.

The North American computer hobbyists' movement was another social factor that contributed to the marginalization of MCM. The computer hobby phenomenon goes back to the second half of the 1960s, when organizations such as the Amateur Computer Society began publishing newsletters to provide electronics hobbyists interested in computing with a forum for exchange of information on computer technology. One of the most influential early publications for computer enthusiasts was *The People's Computer Company* magazine (PCC), published bi-monthly starting in October 1972. PCC portrayed itself as

a newspaper...
about having fun with computers
and   learning how to use computers
and   how to buy a minicomputer for yourself or your school
and   books ... and films ... and tools of the future.[28]

PCC helped to establish BASIC as the "people's" programming language. In its premier issue, PCC wrote, "If you want to talk to computers, you got to learn a language. There are lots of languages talking to computers. Most of them are O.K. for computer freaks but lousy for people. We will use the computer language called BASIC – great for people, not so good for computer freaks."[29]

Until the early 1970s, very few computer amateurs attempted the construction of a computer for their own individual use. However, with the advent of the first commercially available 8-bit microprocessors, the computer hobby movement exploded. Since mid-1974, the hobbyists had been buying, building, and experimenting with rudimentary low-cost microcomputers which were frequently offered to them in do-it-yourself kit form. The capabilities of these early hobby computers were quite limited in comparison with the commercial microcomputers from General Automation, Intel, MCM, or R2E. They could only execute simple programs written in assembly language and, later, in BASIC, while, for instance, the MCM computers could be programmed in APL and Intel's Intellec microcomputers in the PL/M language. But in spite of the evident shortcomings of the hobby computers, it was the hobbyists, and not the commercial microcomputer industry, who in the second half of the 1970s almost exclusively disseminated microcomputer knowledge in society. Organized in clubs and groups, they put together computer conventions, shows, and fests, ran educational programs, and published newsletters. Soon these early microcomputer activities turned into professional software, hardware, publishing, and retail endeavours and formed the infrastructure for the emerging personal microcomputer software and hardware industries. The corporate histories of some of the world's largest microcomputer software and hardware companies, such as Apple Computer, Microsoft, RCA, and Montreal-based Matrox were affected by the hobbyists' movement.

MCM was never interested in the hobby computer market, although in 1976 it presented its computers to the Toronto Region Association of Computer Enthusiasts (TRACE) – one of the earliest computer hobby groups in Canada. TRACE was brought to life in January 1976 by a group of engineers from the Canadian Development Division of Control Data Corporation, located in Mississauga, Ontario. Three months later, several TRACE members formed the TRACE APL special interest group to look for ways to use microcomputers to execute APL programs from the extensive libraries created for mainframe computers.[30] They invited MCM to learn about the company's APL accomplishments. It is likely that MCM accepted TRACE's invitation, no doubt looking for possible sales to some of the corporations that employed the club's members. However, no attempt was made to use TRACE as a gateway to a larger North American market, even after TRACE joined the Midwest Association of Computer Clubs and began a regular exchange of its newsletter with the many member clubs.

From 1976 on, MCM was shifting down its operations from trailblazing innovation to survival mode. It was morphing into a company that was no longer able to anticipate or respond to market and technological trends, a company with deep financial problems and inadequate marketing. Out of synch with the APL movement and unable to profit from either the computer hobby movement or the rapid growth in home and desktop microcomputer markets, MCM was finally relegated to the periphery of computing where the technological collective memory is neither formed nor refreshed. "With the speed of innovation, much is lost in the shuffle," wrote Mike Cassidy in his "Canadian Getting his Due as Pioneer in Computing" article for *The Seattle Times* in October 2003. "Those who survive are remembered. Those who don't, well, maybe not."[31]

For three decades after its introduction, the MCM/70 was exiled from computing history, remaining no more than a footnote to the personal computer narrative. Only sporadic publications acknowledged, sometimes inaccurately, the computer's existence.[32] Then at last, in 2003, the MCM/70 got the chance to reclaim its place in the history of modern computing. The publication of "The Making of the MCM/70 Microcomputer" in the April–June 2003 issue of the *IEEE Annals of the History of Computing* caught the attention of technology commentators and the media.[33] Then on 25 September 2003, *The Globe and Mail* and *The Toronto Star* newspapers published front-page articles to mark the 30th anniversary of the MCM/70's unveiling, retelling the story of the birth of this unique computer.[34] Soon afterwards, media around the world followed suit with their own tributes to the MCM/70. "This homage to the 30th anniversary of Mers Kutt's breakthrough in personal computing is long overdue," wrote Cassidy in his "Never Heard of Mers Kutt, Eh? Time You Did" article for *Mercury News*, San Jose, in October 2003. "The anniversary was last month. I missed it because, well, because I'd never heard of Kutt or his MCM-70 microcomputer. What's that? You'd never heard of them either? Let that be a lesson."

In August 2005, Mers Kutt was appointed to the Order of Canada, the nation's highest honour for lifetime achievements.

MCM TIMELINE

■■■■■□□□

1971
- 30 December: Kutt Systems Inc. incorporated in Toronto; Mers Kutt president; authorized capital $50,000 through 100,000 common shares; company address: 11 Ruden Crescent, Don Mills, Ontario.

1972
- October: José Laraya formally joined Kutt Systems Inc.
- 11 November: The first MCM/70 prototype demonstrated during general shareholders' meeting; motion passed to change the company's name to Micro Computer Machines Inc.
- 28 November: By-law adopted to change the number of MCM directors from one to five.
- December: Venture capital group consisting of Vermay Investments Ltd, B.V. Elliot, W.S. Robertson, and J.T. Johnson purchased 6,290 common shares of Kutt Systems Inc.
- month unknown: Kutt Systems Inc. opened its R&D and manufacturing facility in Kingston, Ontario.

1973
- 3 January: 98,315 issued and 1,685 unissued shares subdivided into 245,787.5 issued and 4,212.5 unissued shares; authorized capital increased to $2,000,000 by creating additional 1,750,000 shares without per value.

- 7 February: W.S. Robertson and M.L. Davies became directors.
- 12 February: MCM's headquarters moved to 4 Lansing Square, Willowdale, Ontario.
- 7 April: M. Kutt signed an agreement with venture capital group that paved a way to $235,000 line of credit from the Toronto Dominion Bank.
- April: Reg Rea joined MCM.
- 15–18 May: An MCM/70 prototype demonstrated during the Fifth International APL Users Conference in Toronto.
- 25 May: W.H. Thomson became director.
- July: E.M. Edwards, G. Seeds, and J. Litchfield joined MCM from Control Data Canada.
- 22–24 August: A briefcase version of the MCM/70 shown during the APL Conference held in Copenhagen, Denmark.
- 10 September: The MCM/70 unveiled at the Canadian High Commission in London, United Kingdom.
- 19–28 September: The MCM/70 shown during the SICOB'73 exhibit in Paris.
- 25 September: The MCM/70 officially unveiled in Toronto.
- 27–28 September: The MCM/70 officially unveiled in New York and Boston.
- 16–18 October: The MCM/70 shown during the Canadian Computer Show & Conference in Toronto.
- October: M. Kutt signed an amendment to the 7 April agreement.

1974
- March: M. Day's critical study *Why we should abandon the TCF project* released; Kutt signed a new agreement with venture capital group calling for an increase of bank line of credit by an additional $180,000; Kutt asked to

forgo his monthly salary of $3,000, effective 1 April 1974, until the production of the MCM/70 was to begin.

- 2 April: B.C. Wallace became director.
- May: Early models of the MCM/70 delivered to distributors.
- 10 June: Kutt relinquished General Manager's duties to Day; the company was in no financial position to hire a new GM.
- 16 July: M. Day, E.M. Edwards, J. Laraya, G. Ramer, R. Rea, M. Smyth, and P. Wolfe met with MCM's board of directors; board amended By-law No. 1 of MCM to strip the office of the president of all effective powers in running the company; board appointed B.C. Wallace managing director of MCM.
- August: Kutt hired P.G. Beattie, a lawyer with the Toronto law firm McCarthy & McCarthy, to represent him in his dispute with venture capital group.
- 1 August: A group of twenty-two MCM employees sent a memo to the board of directors demanding the end to the power supply dispute.
- 16 August: Edwards issued a report on the status of the power supply; his document indicated the power supply completion by 12 September.
- 22 August: MCM/Kutt Agreement proposed to venture capital group rejected.
- 17 September: MCM's trip to its United States distributor ILC Data Device Corporation of Hickville, New York; the number of power supply–related failures in demonstrated MCM/70 computers was alarming.
- 24 September: Group of eighteen MCM employees issued a report on the status of the MCM/70's power supply and the impact of its incompleteness on the company; they called for reinstating Kutt's presidential powers; Kutt

requested board meeting to amend company's By-law
No. 1 and to call general meeting of MCM's shareholders
to elect the company's officers in accordance with the
amended by-law.

- 2 October: MCM announced layoffs.
- 15 October: S. Robertson resigned as director.
- 18 October: Kutt mailed a dramatic letter to shareholders
  looking for their support in his battle against venture
  capital group.
- 21 October: Kutt's presidential powers restored during
  board's meeting.
- 25 October: During a meeting with B.V. Elliot, Kutt
  agreed to resign as president and to sell his controlling
  shares to Elliot, effective 30 October.
- 30 October: Robertson re-joined board of directors.
- 31 October: Kutt resigned as director and president.
- November: First shipments of MCM/70 computers
  equipped with ordinary power supplies to customers.
- month unknown: G. Ramer released his *Micro Computer
  Machines: Development Policy* report on how MCM
  might begin manufacturing the next generation of
  computers by 1975.

1975

- 18 April: T.M. Berg replaced M.L. Davies as director.
- 1 May: T.M. Berg appointed MCM's president and
  Robertson the company's secretary.
- June: SYSMO S.A. set up in Paris to distribute MCM
  computers in France.
- September: The MCM/700 shown during the Brno
  International Trade Fair, Czechoslovakia.
- November: The MCM/700 shown during the Moscow
  Trade Fair, USSR.

- month unknown: Regular production and routine customer shipments of the MCM/700 begun in the first half of 1975; 150 MCM/700s delivered by the end of 1975.

1976
- 21 June: Number of MCM directors increased to six; T.C. Grunau became director.
- July: The MCM/800 announced.

1977
- 11 January: W.H. Thompson ceased to be director.
- 1 March: C.M. Williams became director.
- 12 April: Berg replaced by Williams as president.
- 24 June: William H. Thomson became director.
- June: MCM changed its name from Micro Computer Machines Inc. to MCM Computers Ltd.
- July: Number of directors increased from six to seven.
- month unknown: MCM headquarters moved to 6700 Finch Ave West, Suite 600, Rexdale, Ontario.

1978
- 8 June: Number of directors increased from seven to nine. Anthony Knox, Rene Remy (Switzerland), Rodolphe Pfander (Switzerland), and Alain LePoullouin (France) became directors; authorized capital of MCM increased from $2 million to $5 million by the creation of an additional 3 million shares.
- 7 July: Knox ceased to be director.
- 18 August: W.H. Thomson ceased to be director.
- September: The MCM/900 announced.
- 11 October: Salim Hameer became a director.

1979

- 15 January: George Kyle and James H. Finch replaced T.C. Grunau and S. Hameer as directors.
- 13–15 November: The MCM/900 showed during the Canadian Computer Show in Toronto.
- 15 December: B.J.F. Woods replaced Williams as president and CEO.

1980

- month unknown: The MCM Power and MicroPower computers announced; MCM displayed the MCM Power and MicroPower computers at the COMPEC'80 computer show in London, United Kingdom; British firm BL Systems Ltd appointed to distribute MCM computers in the United Kingdom.
- 11–13 November: The MCM/900 and Power computers displayed during the Canadian Computer Show in Toronto.

1981

- 23 February: C.M. Williams replaced by Willis S. McLeese as director.
- 27 April: Wallace ceased to be a director; Ken Shaw appointed secretary and treasurer.
- 14 May: MCM issued additional 1,5668,033 shares.
- August: Company's headquarters moved to 6815 Rexwood Rd, Units 9 and 10, Mississauga, Ontario.

1982

- January: Woods bought two-thirds of MCM shares.
- 11 March: Robertson ceased to be a director.
- 28 June: MCM terminated the offices of president and secretary.

- 30 June: MCM's board of directors dissolved.
- June: MCM foreclosed.

1985
- 15 May: Ontario Ministry of Consumer and Commercial Relations sent a notice of dissolution to MCM.

NOTES

INTRODUCTION

1 Cf. Ceruzzi, *A History of Modern Computing*, 224.
2 Cf. Stachniak, "Intel SIM8-01: A Proto-PC"; see also Stachniak, "The MIL MF7114 Microprocessor."

CHAPTER ONE

1 Cf. *Canadian Computer Census 1973*, 18.
2 Interview with Gord Ramer. Henceforth, unless stated otherwise, all unreferenced quotations have been obtained during interviews I conducted for this book.
3 Cf. Mason, "Kenneth Iverson: From a Symbolic Notation to A Programming Language."
4 Iverson, "Notation as a Tool of Thought," 444–65.
5 Apart from York University, which supported York APL until 1977, Ramer's APL was used, among other places, by Simon Fraser University, Ryerson Polytechnical Institute, University of Rochester in Rochester, NY, Northern European University Computer Centre in Copenhagen, Denmark, Statistics Canada, and West Virginia Network.

CHAPTER TWO

1 Cf. Vhevreau, "The Third Coming of Mers Kutt," 112–15.
2 Cf. Bleackley and LaPrairie, *Entering the Computer Age. The Computer Industry in Canada: The First Thirty Years*, 54–6.
3 Cf. "Micro Computer Machines Inc.: Giving Canada World Lead."
4 Cf. Berkeley and Jensen, "World's Smallest Electric Brain," 29–30.

5 Cf. Weisbecker, *Computer Coin Games: Educational Fun for Every-one* and *Home Computers Can Make You Rich.*

6 Cf. Weisbecker, *The* FRED *System.*

7 Cf. Weisbecker, "Build the COSMAC 'ELF': A Low Cost Experiment-er's Microcomputer."

8 Intel's August 1974 price list shows the P1101 RAM chip at $6.50 apiece and the P2101 RAM chip (employed in the MCM/70) at the reduced price of $15.40 apiece, in quantities of one hundred and over.

CHAPTER THREE

1 Cf. "Announcing a new era in integrated electronics, a microprogram-mable computer on a chip!" Intel's advertisement in *Electronic News*, 15 November 1971.

2 Cf. MCS-8 *Micro Computer Set. 8008: 8 Bit Parallel Central Proces-sor Unit Users Manual.*

3 The Teletype Model ASR-33 was a electromechanical typewriter intro-duced in the early 1960s by Teletype Corporation. It was a very pop-ular terminal used, among other applications, to communicate with mainframes and minicomputers. The ASR-33 could send data stored on a paper tape and store data on such a tape using a built-in paper tape reader and tape punch.

4 In the early 1970s, Burroughs Corporation introduced a new genera-tion of flat panel displays called the Self-Scan. The panels used gas dis-charge glow cavities (or dots) to display information. Self-Scans were capable of displaying numeric, alphanumeric, or graphic information in a dot matrix format (using 4-dot-wide by 7-dot-high matrix). Cf. *Self-Scan Panel Display.*

5 Cf. Friedl, "SCAMP: The Missing Link in the PC's Past?", 190–7.

6 MCM sales records, 1975.

7 Cf. Bleackley and LaPrairie, *Entering the Computer Age. The Com-puter Industry in Canada: The First Thirty Years*, 118.

8 For those readers who are not familiar with APL, the expand operator "\", as used in "APL\360", and the contraction operator "/", as used in "MCM/APL", allow a user to expand and contract APL data objects called vectors.

9 Cf. MCM *User's Guide*, Introduction.

10 "UPS" stands for "Uninterruptible Power System."

11 Cf. MCM/70 *User's Guide*, 243.

CHAPTER FOUR

1 Cf. "Mers Kutt Planning New Computer Firm," 58.
2 *Canadian Datasystems*, March 1973, 58 and 81.
3 *Canadian Datasystems*, August 1973, 13.
4 For more information on Control Data Canada, see Vardalas, *The Computer Revolution in Canada. Building National Technological Competence.*
5 From e-mail correspondence between Ted Edwards and Ned Chapin, 2002. By permission of Ned Chapin.
6 Cf. "Sensationele nieuwe computer uit Canada," "Eine neue Computer-Generation," and "Desktop Model from Canada will Operate on Mains or Batteries." Other newspaper articles reporting on the MCM/70 are listed in Bibliography.
7 Cf. Bul, "Un miniordinateur pour moins de 8500FF."
8 The Canadian representative for R2E's products was Fortin Electronics Corporation with offices in Winnipeg, Manitoba, and Downsview, Ontario.
9 Johnston, "In Search of Techne."
10 Cf. *The Globe and Mail*, 26 September 1973; *The Toronto Star*, 27 September 1973; *Canadian Datasystems*, October 1973; *The Wall Street Journal*, 28 September 1973; *Financial Times*, 1 October 1973; *The Financial Post*, 6 October 1973; *Computerworld*, 10 October and 7 November 1973.
11 *EDP Daily*, 1 October 1973.
12 From the 1973 MCM/70 *Desk Top Computer* promotional brochure.
13 From the 1974 MCM/700 promotional brochure.

CHAPTER SIX

1 Thomas, *Knights of the New Technology. The Inside Story of Canada's Computer Elite*, 96.

CHAPTER SEVEN

1 See also "Portable APL Machine" in ACM APL *Quote Quad* and in *Datapro Newscom*.
2 See Linzmayer, *Apple Confidential: The Real Story of Apple Computer Inc.*, 46–7.

3 Cf. Osborne, *The Value of Micropower: A Microcomputer Handbook.*
4 Cf. Minnich, "MCM Computers Sees Bright Future in Desk-top APL," 68 and 70.

CONCLUSIONS

1 Cf. "Kleiner Canadier" and "Sensationele nieuwe computer uit Canada."
2 Cf. Stachniak, "Intel SIM8-01: A proto-PC," 34–48.
3 Cf. "Micro Computer Machines Inc.: Giving Canada World Lead," *Electronics Communicator.*
4 Cf. "Computer Operates with Calculator Ease," 45.
5 From MCM *Media/Press Release,* 28 September 1973.
6 Cf. MCM/70 *Introductory Manual,* 27.
7 Cf. Aldrich Kidwell, "'Yours for Improvement' – The Adding Machines of Chicago, 1884–1930."
8 From a 1893 advertisement of the Ribbon Adder, Ribbon Adder, 167 Broadway, NY.
9 From the 1975 MCM/700 promotional brochure.
10 Cf. Day, MCM/70 *Introductory Manual,* 27.
11 These terms were used, for instance, in the 1975 MCM/700 promotional brochure.
12 From the 1973 MCM/70 *Desk Top Computer* promotional brochure.
13 From the MCM/700 promotional brochure, 6.
14 Cf. Day, MCM/70 *Introductory Manual,* 2.
15 Cf. "Digital Computer Kenbak-1," announcement in *Scientific American,* September 1971, 194.
16 Glenn Schneider, personal communication, 2001.
17 Harley Courtney, personal communication, 2003.
18 Cf. Polivka, "Lingo Allegro USA Inc. Partners: Andrei Kondrashev, Walter Fil, and Steve Halasz," 13–17.
19 From MCM's confidential letter to A. Carr, Director of Electronics Branch, Department of Industry, Trade & Commerce, 20 February 1973.
20 Cf. Linzmayer, *Apple Confidential. The Real Story of Apple Computer Inc.,* 13.
21 By 1979, the MCM software library included programs such as a text editor, Client Accounting, Financial Accounting, and General Ledger.

22 The Apple][was priced at $1,298 on introduction. In 1978, Apple introduced the Disk][floppy drive at $495 a drive.

23 As opposed to MCM, R2E never hid the fact that its Micral used the Intel 8008 microprocessor.

24 Cf. Brown, "APL at the Crossroads."

25 Cf. "APL: Good For The Brain"; see also Posa, "APL makes splash in small computers."

26 In fall of 1975, *ACM APL Quote Quad* – the main journal devoted to APL – published a two-page article on the occasion of the IBM 5100's introduction. Following this article, the editors invited MCM/70 users to share their experiences with a portable APL environment. In spite of many important installations of the MCM/70 computers, MCM failed to arrange and publish even a survey of some of the applications done on MCM computers in the journal.

27 The Commodore SuperPET developed at the University of Waterloo in the early 1980s was one such computer. It was equipped with the University of Waterloo's microAPL interpreter.

28 Cf. *People's Computer Company* 1, no. 1 (1972), 1.

29 Cf. *People's Computer Company* 1, no. 1 (1972), 5.

30 Several TRACE members had considerable APL expertise. One of the software projects at CDC was the implementation of an APL interpreter for the Star-65 computer. That project was led by Ted Edwards, but after his departure for MCM, the project was completed by TRACE member William Kindree.

31 Cf. Cassidy, "Silicon Valley View: Canadian Getting his Due as Pioneer in Computing" and "Never Heard of Mers Kutt, Eh? Time You Did."

32 In their book *Entering the Computer Age. The Computer Industry in Canada: The First Thirty Years*, Bleackley and LaPrairie incorrectly identify the "MCM 800 desktop computer" as the first MCM computer.

33 Cf. Stachniak, "The Making of the MCM/70 Microcomputer"; see also Stachniak, "The MCM/70 Microcomputer."

34 Cf. Alphonso, "Canadian Hailed as Father of the PC" and Ross, "Remembering the MCM/70."

BIBLIOGRAPHY

■■■■■■■■■

Aldrich Kidwell, P. "'Yours for Improvement' – The Adding Machines of Chicago, 1884–1930." *IEEE Annals of the History of Computing* 23, no. 3 (July 2001): 3–21.

Alphonso, C. "Canadian Hailed as Father of the PC." *The Globe and Mail*, 25 September 2003.

Berkeley, E. *Giant Brains; Or, Machines That Think*. New York, London: John Wiley & Sons, Inc. 1949.

Berkeley, E., and Jensen, R.E. "World's Smallest Electric Brain; Relays Do Simple Arithmetic; How an Electric Brain Works." *Radio Electronics*, October 1950–October 1951.

Bleackley, B.J., and LaPrairie, J. *Entering the Computer Age. The Computer Industry in Canada: The First Thirty Years*. Agincourt: The Book Society of Canada Ltd 1982.

Brown, R.G. "APL at the Crossroads." *APL89 Conference Proceedings*, Kertesz A. and Shaw, L.C., eds, ACM Press, *APL Quote Quad* 19, no. 4 (August 1989): 68–74.

Bul, R. "Un miniordinateur pour moins de 8500FF." *zero.un.informatique hebdo* 228, 12 February 1973: 1 and 5.

Canadian Computer Census 1973. Canadian Information Processing Society 1973.

Cassidy, M. "Silicon Valley View: Canadian Getting his Due as Pioneer in Computing." *The Seattle Times*, 13 October 2003.

– "Never Heard of Mers Kutt, Eh? Time You Did." *Mercury News*, San Jose, 9 October 2003.

Ceruzzi, P.E. *A History of Modern Computing*. Cambridge, London: MIT Press 1998.

Chevreau, J. "The Third Coming of Mers Kutt." *Report on Business Magazine*, November 1985: 110–15.

Day, M. MCM/70 *Introductory Manual*. Toronto: Micro Computer Machines 1973.

Friedl, P.J. "SCAMP: The Missing Link in the PC's Past?" *PC Magazine*, November 1983: 190–7.

Gjerløv, P., Helms, H.J., and Nielsen, J., eds. *APL Congress 73. Proceedings of the APL Congress 73*. Copenhagen, Denmark, 22–24 August 1973. North-Holland 1973.

Iverson, K.E. "Notation as a Tool of Thought." *Communications of the ACM* 23, no. 8 (1980): 444–65.

– *A Programming Language*. New York, London: John Wiley & Sons, Inc. 1962.

Johnston, R. "In Search of Techne." *Century of Endeavour. The Irish Times Science and Technology Column*, 2002. http://www.iol.ie/~rjtechne/itimes/itimes70.htm

Linzmayer, O.W. *Apple Confidential: The Real Story of Apple Computer Inc*. San Francisco: No Starch Press 1999.

Mason, J.F. "Kenneth Iverson: From a Symbolic Notation to A Programming Language." *Electronic Design*, 7 June 1977.

MCM/70 *User's Guide*. Toronto: Micro Computer Machines 1974.

MCM *News* 1, issue 1 (1975).

MCS-8 *Micro Computer Set. 8008: 8 Bit Parallel Central Processor Unit Users Manual*. Intel Corp. (March 1973).

Minnich, M. "MCM Computers Sees Bright Future in Desk-top APL." *Canadian Datasystems*, March 1979: 68 and 70.

Moore, L.B. (chair). *Proceedings of the Fifth International APL Users' Conference*. Toronto, Canada, 15–18 May 1973, APL Technical Committee 1973.

Osborne, A., & Associates, Inc. *The Value of Micropower: A Microcomputer Handbook*. Anaheim: General Automation 1974.

Polivka, R. "Lingo Allegro USA Inc. Partners: Andrei Kondrashev, Walter Fil, and Steve Halasz." *APL Quote Quad* 30, no. 2, December 1999: 13–17.

Posa, J.G. "APL Makes Splash in Small Computers." *Electronics*, 21 December 1978: 68–9.

Ramer, G. *York APL Users Guide*. Toronto: APL Systems, 15 November 1971.

Ross, R. "Remembering the MCM/70." *The Toronto Star*, 25 September 2003.

Self-Scan Panel Display. Theory of Operations. Burroughs Application Notes, S101A, 1971.

Smyth, J.M. *York APL*. Toronto: Ryerson Polytechnical Institute 1972.

Spanjaard, E., and Della-Mussia, J-P. "Le Microprocesseur: un outil suprenant, difficile à connaître." *Inter Électronique*, no. 114 (November 1973): 28–33.

Stachniak, Z. "The MIL MF7114 Microprocessor." *IEEE Annals of the History of Computing* 32, no. 4 (October–December 2010): 48–59.

– "Intel SIM8-01: A Proto-PC." *IEEE Annals of the History of Computing* 29, no. 1 (January–March 2007): 34–48.

– "The Making of the MCM/70 Microcomputer." *IEEE Annals of the History of Computing* 25, no. 2 (April–June 2003): 62–75.

– "The MCM/70 Microcomputer." *Core 4.1*, The Computer History Museum (September 2003): 6–12.

Stachniak, Z., and Campbell, S.M. *Computing in Canada: Building a Digital Future*. Ottawa: Canada Science and Technology Museum, *Transformation Series 17*, 2009.

Thomas, D. *Knights of the New Technology. The Inside Story of Canada's Computer Elite*. Toronto: Key Porter Books 1983.

Vardalas, J.N. *The Computer Revolution in Canada. Building National Technological Competence*. Cambridge, London: The MIT Press 2001.

Weisbecker, J. *Home Computers Can Make You Rich*. Hayden Book Co. 1980.

– *Computer Coin Games: Educational Fun for Everyone*. Creative Computing Press 1979.

– "A Practical Low-Cost, Home/School Microprocessor System." *IEEE Computer* (August 1974): 20–31.

– "Build the COSMAC 'ELF': A Low Cost Experimenter's Microcomputer." *Popular Electronics*, Part I (August 1976), Part II (September 1976), Part III (March 1977).

– *An Eight-Bit Micro-Processor*. RCA technical report PRRL-71-TR-207 (1971).

Weinstein, M., and Leavitt, D. "APL-dedicated Microprocessor Has 16K Memory, Weighs 20lbs." *Computerworld*, 10 October 1973: 1–2.

Wiseman, T. "APL-compatible Devices Lead New Products at Canadian Show." *Computerworld*, 7 November 1973: 1.

Woods, B.J.F. "APL Makes for More Powerful Micros." *Computing Canada*, 5 August 1980: 16–17.

Anonymous newspaper and magazine articles quoted in this book and arranged alphabetically

"All-Canadian Company Unveils Unique Microcomputer." *The Electronics Communicator* 4, no. 19 (1 October 1973): 1 and 5.

"APL for Teachers ... With 16–22K Bytes!" *Datamation*, November 1973: 153.

"APL: Good for the Brain." *ETI Canada*, March 1979: 22–9.

"BASIC! Or, U2 Can Control a Computer." *The People's Computer Company* 1, no. 1 (October 1972): 5.

"Canadees komt met portable computer." *De Telegraaf*, 29 August 1973.

"Computer i en kuffert." *Politiken*, 23 August 1973: 1 and 20.

"Computer Operates with Calculator Ease." *Machine Design* 45, 29 November 1973: 14.

"Computer Show." *The Financial Post*, 29 September 1973.

"Desk Computer Doubles as Terminal." *Electronic Engineering Times*, 5 November 1973.

"Desk-top Computer." *Automation*, November 1973.

"Desktop Model from Canada Will Operate on Mains or Batteries." *The Times*, 11 September 1973: 21.

"Digital Computer Kenbak-1." Announcement in *Scientific American*. September 1971: 194.

"Eine neue Computer-Generation." BRD, 30 August 1973.

"Kleiner Canadier," *Wirtschaftswoche* 40, 28 September 1973: 90.

"Kutt Returns with Micro Computer Ltd." *Canadian Datasystems*, March 1973: 61.

"Kutt Takes Wraps Off New Minicomputer." *Canadian Datasystems*, October 1973: 49.

"MCM-Chef Mers Kutt: Computerbau-Revolution." *Die Computer Zeitung*, October 1973.

"MCM 70: Revolution in APL." *Online*, October 1973.

"Mers Kutt Is Back with Minicomputers." *Canadian Datasystems*, August 1973: 13.

"Mers Kutt Shows His Portable Computer." *Canadian Information Processing Society (CIPS)*, November 1973: 9.

"Mers Kutt Planning New Computer Firm." *Canadian Datasystems*, March 1972: 58.

"Micro Computer." *The Globe and Mail*, 26 September 1973: 86.

"Micro computer Adds Terminal." *Electronic News* 18, no. 944, 8 October 1973: 59.

"Micro Computer Machines Inc., Introduced What It Calls 'World's First Portable APL Computer.'" *EDP Daily*, 1 October 1973: 1.

"Micro Computer Machines ontwikkelt MCM/70 gebaseerd op APL programmering." *Informatie*, October 1973.

"A Microcomputer to Bypass the Compiler." *Electronics and Communications* 31, no. 8 (1973): 7.

"Un 'mini' canadien functionnant en APL." *électronique actualités* (Paris) 297, 21 September 1973.

"Un ordinateur de bureau qui parle APL." *Inter Électronique*, 17 September 1973: 32 and 35.

"Portable APL Machine." *Datapro Newscom* 3, no. 10 (October 1975).

"Portable APL Machine." *ACM APL Quote Quad* 6, no. 3 (fall 1975): 9–10.

"Portable Computer." *The Office – Magazine of Management, Equipment, Automation*, November 1973.

"Portable Microcomputer with APL Language Offers Large Computing Power." *Computer Design* 12, no. 11 (November 1973): 122–3.

"Product/Processes: Micro Computer Machines." *The Financial Times*, 1 October 1973: 24.

"Schlauer Besuch." *Frankfurter Rundschau*, 3 September 1973: 3.

"Sensationele nieuwe computer uit Canada." *Computable* 51, 6 September 1973: 1.

"Le SICOB a bien montré le role grandissant de la péri-informatique." *électronique actualités* (Paris) 299, 5 October 1973: 1–9.

"A Small Computer that Can Operate by Itself Is Shown." *The Wall Street Journal*, 28 September 1973: 3.

"Suitcase-sized Computer." *The Toronto Star*, 27 September 1973: C8.

"Timing May Be Right for New Computer." *The Financial Post*, 6 October 1973: 44.

"$3500 Computer Smaller than a Typewriter." *Administrative Digest*, November 1973.

"$3,500 Minicomputer Is 'Novice Operable.'" *Santa Clara Register*, October 1973.

"$3,500 Minicomputer Unveiled in NY." *Los Angeles Area Newspaper*, October 1973.

"Welturaufführung eines Microcomputers in Deutschland: Wird MCM 70 den Computerbau während der nächsten fünf Jahre revolutionieren?" *Der Erfolg*, October 1973.

INDEX

Graham, Wesley, 13
Gray, Stephen, 35
Grunau, T.C., 193–4

Halifax Insurance, 148
Hameer, Salim, 193–4
Harvard University, 14; Automated
Data Processing Program, 14;
Computation Laboratory, 14;
Mark I, II, III, and IV calcula-
tors, 14
Hewlett-Packard, 74, 140, 177; 9830
programmable calculator, 74, 143
Hoff, Marcian (Ted), Jr, 40–1, 43
Honeywell Controls Ltd, 23, 25, 157

I.P. Sharp Associates Ltd, 60, 148,
155, 176
IBM: 610 computer, 13; 1570 computer (Elsie), 140; 1620 computer,
23–5; 1622 card read punch, 23–4;
5100 computer, 52, 140–3, 152,
155, 174, 176–7, 182, 184, 201;
5110 computer, 152, 155; Personal
Computer (PC), 142, 162; Special
Computer, APL Machine Portable, 52, 140; System\360, 25, 77;
System\360 Model 40 computer,
19, 25; System\360 Model 50
computer, 25; System\370 Models
158 and 168, 61–2
IBM Canada, 22
IBM Corporation, 12, 16, 19, 25,
51–2, 134, 137, 139–43, 149–52,
155, 162, 165, 176–7, 182, 184;
General Systems Division, Atlanta,
52, 140; Scientific Center, Palo
Alto, 52, 140; Watson Research
Center, Yorktown Heights, 12
ILC Data Device Corporation, 110–
11, 114, 138–9, 180, 191
Innocean Investments Ltd, 134–5
Intel Corporation, 4–5, 11, 29,
36–43, 48, 53–4, 87–8, 165, 186,
198; 1101 RAM, 36; 2102 RAM,

36; 4004 microprocessor, 36–7,
40–2; 4004 μ-Computer, 41–3;
8008 microprocessor, 5, 12,
18–19, 36–7, 42–5, 47–8, 53–4,
56–8, 67, 70–1, 84, 86, 88, 135,
139, 144, 153–4, 181, 201; 8080
microprocessor, 70, 72, 82, 85–91,
136, 146–7, 181, 184–5; 8080A
microprocessor, 91; Applications
Research Group, 38–41, 43; Intellec computers, 4, 186; Micro
Computer Systems Group, 41;
MP7-01 EPROM programmer,
41; MP7-02 EPROM program-
mer, 43–4, 56; PL/M language,
186; SIM4-01 prototyping system,
40–1, 43; SIM8-01 prototyping
system, 43–4, 48–9
Interactive Computer Systems Inc,
150
Iverson, Kenneth, 12–18; notation,
14–16

Johnson, J.T., 92
Joubert, M., 71

Kemeny, John, 135
Kenbak Corporation, 173
Kenbak-1 educational computer, 173
Key-Cassette prototype, 29–30
Key-Edit Falcon, 27
Key-Edit 100, 26
key-edit system, 26–7, 30
Kindree, William, 201
Knox, Anthony, 193
Kondrashev, Andrei, 175
KSI, see Kutt Systems Incorporated
Kurtz, Thomas, 135
Kutt, Merslau (Mers), 4–7, 9–12,
18–19, 21–3, 25–9, 35–7, 41–4,
46–8, 52–4, 65–6, 68–70, 74–5,
77–8, 80, 86, 89, 92–109, 113–37,
139, 157, 169, 182, 188–92
Kutt Systems Incorporated, 21, 28,
38, 41–6, 48–9, 54, 56, 92–3